AN ARTIST'S JOURNEY

Margaret
Bialokoz
Margaret
Malgorzata
Malga
Malgorzata
Tilgner
Tilgner
Tilgner
Margaret
Bialokoz
Malgorzata
Malga
Bialokoz
Smith
Tilgner
Tilgner
Bialokoz
.smith
Malgorzata
Bialokoz
Tilgner
Smith

An Artist's Journey

MALGORZATA BIALOKOZ SMITH

Oxford Publishing Services

Published in 2016 by

Oxford Publishing Services

34 Warnborough Road

Oxford

OX2 6JA

ISBN: 978 0 9550031 5 8

Typeset in Garamond by Oxford Publishing Services

Printed by CPI Group (UK) Ltd, Croyden CRO 4YY

Contents

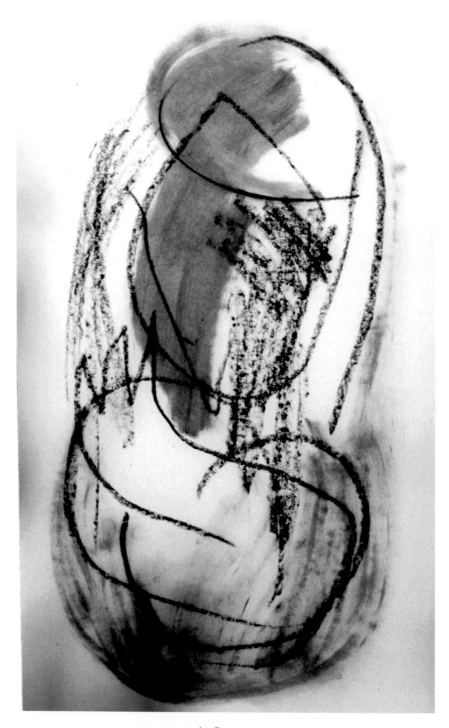

La Donna

Preface

At the age of 78 it is time to be in earnest
Samuel Johnson

To write a memorial is to recall the past time and space in which the events of one's life took place. Memory is a device for remembering as well as forgetting. To look back at one's life is to experience the capriciousness of memory. For me the events which I remember are like pictures, some in glorious, happy colours; others in dramatic blacks and greys. Every life story is different and is influenced by historical events, the family, its culture and tradition. All this is part of "providential accident". My story is divided into two very different parts. First one takes place in Poland during the war and the subsequent Russian occupation and the second one, much longer in time, in England.

I was fortunate to have exceptional parents who nurtured my development and instilled in me their philosophy of life based on great resilience and strength of spirit. The war did not destroy their humanity and ability to find solutions to many problems of the postwar, destructive political system in Poland.

The second part of my life in England taught me about democracy. This is the world which is characterised by respect, dignity, compassion and above all, the freedom of speech. Human achievements are rewarded, individuality and originality applauded. Ambition, hard work and a network of good friends made my life fulfilling.

The process of reviewing my life and writing about it was both – happy and sad. Happy were the times of achievement in art and seeing my children grow up and reach their potential. Sad, because the mistakes which I made cannot be rectified and the tragedies through which I had to live were always unexpected. These are the black periods in my art but it is my hope that I managed to achieve a poetic and balanced vision of life. The story written in words is the factual part of an autobiography, easy to understand while the art produced over many years is the other, equally important one requiring more involvement and interpretation.

Malgorzata

1. Parents and the War

My life's journey began on September in year 1937 in the elegant and stylish city of Warsaw, Poland. My birth at that date and in that particular clinic was going to change my life dramatically 20 years later. Accidental providence brought together two women who gave

Eleonora and Antony Hauffe

My mother, Halina, aged 4.

birth at the same time and in the same clinic. Maria and Halina, my mother, became friends as did the two new fathers Tadeusz and Damazy my father. The birth of a baby is a life changing experience for both parents. Halina and Damazy from the moment of my birth, throughout their long life, gave me their unconditional support and love.

Family Tilgner on holiday before the First World War

Hauffe father with my mother on the right, Uncle Ric on the left and Aunt Zula on the lap

*My parents' engagement,
August 1935*

I am not sure why I was given the name Malgorzata, difficult to pronounce hence throughout my life I acquired variations like Malga, Gosia and later Margaret.

In her twenties, my mother had travelled to America and worked as a secretary in the Polish consulate in Chicago. In the evenings at weekends she gave language lessons to maximise her income. She planned to build a house for her family upon return to Poland. She spoke four languages and literature was her great passion. Her intelligence and beauty made her popular on the social scene of Chicago.

My father worked in food science and technology and in 1928 he went to America to work first in Ohio in a canning Company and the famous Armour and Company in Chicago. Being a foreigner he was often challenged with the hardest jobs within the factories. He was a sportsman since his student's days, a first class rower winning many championships at home, in Europe and in the USA. Physical fitness, gave him strength and resilience to perform demanding tasks in many situations in his long life. On his journey home, he worked his passage on the ship by painting the ships iron and wood work. In the evenings during the voyage he was writing his first text book *Modern Canning Industry*. While in Chicago he was told about a beautiful Polish woman, Halina, who became a social celebrity. Damazy was determined to

*The two sisters, (my mother in the middle)
with my father, 1936 Gdynia*

find her upon his return to Poland. My mother told me about the time she met my father: "I was working in my office in Gdansk when a very tall and handsome, smiling man walked in and my heart started beating very fast." This was the beginning of a great romance. They married in August 1935. The house which my mother built for her family was on a hill looking out to sea in the port city of Gdynia, on the Baltic Coast. It was called Villa Damazy. Meanwhile my father was doing research on the subject of food technology for which he became well known. In 1934 he wrote the first book in Poland on food packaging.

While he was in the USA whenever there was a chance he indulged in his passion for rowing and in 1929 became a champion of Golden Gates Singles in California. Between 1931 and 1932 he worked as a manager of modernisation in Konserven Fabric in Potsdam, Germany. In May 1939 he attended a conference in Dresden. He became known among colleges in Germany and the USA. These contacts had unforeseen results at a later time. He did not know that four months later Germany would once more invade Poland. Hitler – a little man, once a shy boy who loved painting and made a living selling these watercolours – ordered an annihilation of the Polish nation.

The area of Warsaw in which our house stood was separated from the centre by the Vistula River. Our suburb was called Saska Kempa. The streets were lined with trees and each villa had a spacious garden. Our house was very strange and ugly. There was not a single window facing the street and the walls were covered with grey pebbledash. On the side stood an equally ugly and grey garage. Many years later while visiting

Our house in Warsaw

Christmas visit from   *My father and his*
Father Christmas, 1940   *daughters in Warsaw*

my uncle and aunt in Warsaw, I visited the house and was invited by the people who bought it from my father after the war when it was very damaged by shelling and virtually roofless. A charming old couple told me that they paid $2000 for it. These banknotes, my father sealed in a tin for safety. Many, many years later he told us the story and when Alexander was in his teens, my father opened

Postcard with Malgorzata,
aged 4 (front and back)

the tin and gave him $100. Alexander was going with his volleyball team to Portugal and took the $100 note with him. When he tried to change it at the bank, he was accused of trying to cheat because the banknote seem to be outdated. Poor Alexander was most embarrassed and tried to make the clerk understand that it was a gift from his grandfather.

It was very moving for me to stand in the old house in which most of the war years were spent. The back of the house had many windows which looked onto a spacious terrace and the garden which now looked small. I remembered the fruit trees, the lawn and the flowerbeds lined with my mother's favourite tall rudbeckias. While my mother sat on the terrace, usually working on some translations, my father played games with me on the lawn. Often, we had to sing some verses while dancing and he was very proud that I had good memory from very early age. These moments were recorded by my father and supported by photographs that miraculously survived the war.

The German war machine demolished most of the central city of Warsaw. During the occupation Poles created underground schools. University courses were taking place in the basements hidden from the German eyes. Secret army and underground defence was active throughout the war. My father belonged to the underground

The Human Story, the Reality of War, *300 x 100 cm, on paper, 1990*

resistance movement under the name Jaromil. When food became
very scarce, women travelled to the outskirts of Warsaw to buy
anything they could from the farmers. Germans imposed strict rules
about everything and everyday life was a fight for survival. For
example it was forbidden to sell white bread! Signs were put up in
the streets and under such notices old women in defiance sold white
bread. The bravery and the spirit of resistance among dwindling
Polish population lasted throughout the war. Many years later my
father told me the following story. He was returning from work on
his bicycle and overtook a tramway full of people returning from
work. Turning the corner, he saw in the distance German trucks
which were being loaded with rounded up men. He immediately
turned back, stopped the tramway and warned its passengers. In
great haste the tramway emptied and everybody ran into the nearest
buildings. He managed, at least for the moment, to save lives. There
were two hiding places in our house. One was in the attic and the
other in the cellar under the mount of coal. Underneath the coal,
was a box big enough for my father to enter through the garden
window and curl up inside like a cat. Germans made regular searches
of people's houses to arrest men. My memory goes back to an
incident when two Germans poked bayonets into that heap of coal
suspecting a hiding place. I was standing with my mother holding
her hand which was very sweaty and I was very afraid in spite of not
understanding what it all meant. It was lucky that the bayonets did
not reach the box. The second hiding space was behind the panelling
in the attic. It was big enough for two people and there Mr and Mrs
Minz, a Jewish couple, stayed hidden for some weeks until the time
when they made a decision to make their way to North-East Poland.
This was the time when the Jewish population of Warsaw was
rounded up, put in ghettos and gradually deported to the
concentration camps. They lived in the ghettos without much food
in barbaric conditions. Some Jews managed to escape, others found
helpful Poles who hid them endangering their own lives. We never
discovered if the Minzes survived and found their way to freedom.

My father told me that to survive in the war, one needed good luck and the knowledge of the German language. Both my parents lived as children in Pozen [Poznan] which was under the German rule. All schools were in German while Polish language was taught in secret, in hidden locations.

The following story was one such proof of how the language helped my father. He was visiting his doctor and while in the surgery a screeching of the big trucks outside in the street meant that another roundup of men was about to take place. The doctor promptly told my father to lie down on the couch and covered him up to his chin. A sweaty and obviously tired German rushed in and before he said anything, my father addressed him in perfect German commiserating with him. The man took his helmet off and wiped the sweat from his forehead. He appreciated my father's concern and asked what was wrong with my father. The doctor span a story about some injury, the man saluted, wished my father speedy recovery and left. Luck and cool composure were paying rewards sometimes.

There is an entry in my father's diary: "today we run out of food". The Germans intensified arrests of men, and father spends a lot of time in hiding. A knock on the door can mean another search and dreadful fear but this time the officer saluted my mother and handed her a big box of food products. He explained that he had met my father before the war when they both worked in a food processing company in Potsdam. Such an unexpected gift from the enemy was proof that even in the time of human barbarity it's possible to come across true humanity. The name of the man was Dr G. Ruppel and my parents knew that he was endangering himself by helping Poles. In 1979 my father went on a visit to Potsdam and met Dr Ruppel once again to reminisce about the war and thank him for saving us from starvation.

My father (left), his brother Wladyslaw with his wife Fela and their three children. I am in front of my grandmother. Aunt Mira and her son, Olgierd, are on the right

My father's brother, Wladyslaw, was wounded at the beginning of the war and discharged from the army. He had a degree in agriculture and found employment as an administrator of the estates of Count Lubomirski, 50 km from Warsaw. His wife and three children were still in Poznan in their home hoping to join him at some stage. Before they managed to join their father, Germans ordered all Poles to leave their homes with basic belongings within one hour. My aunt's youngest child was in the pram and the two other children were of school age and so could carry a small amount of belongings. With hundreds other families, they were loaded onto cattle trains without any knowledge of the destination. For a few days the train moved, day and night, until it suddenly stopped in the middle of nowhere and they were ordered to get out. In the distance they could see some lights of a town. Everybody, however exhausted, walked towards it in hope of some humanity, water and perhaps food. During the cataclysmic events like war, people often helped each other and so it was now. A doctor's wife told her husband to go out and look for any woman who is with a baby and bring her to their house. My aunt found a shelter, kindness and empathy. All four of them were taken care of and in time found their way to their father where a new life could begin. They stayed there till the end of the war. At some stage of the war all of us ended up on that huge farm estate and I met my cousins, saw for the first time horses and other animals. I think that the nature of the countryside must have had a special impact on my life from these early experiences.

The books with fairy stories were my favourite toys and I learned from a very early age to recite some verses and I was eager to entertain anybody who was prepared to listen. Around the age of four I did my first drawing; alas, not a welcome one. A visitor left her handbag on my parents' bed which was covered with a pure white, heavy lace bed cover. While my parents were talking to the visitor in the sitting room, I sneaked out and emptied the contents of the bag and picked up one object which looked like a crayon. In fact it was a bright red lipstick. With it, I drew happily on the white bed cover. I do not recall the reaction of my parents when I was discovered.

Our house has lost its roof from heavy shelling and my parents decided to sell it. The year was 1945 and Poland from now on will be under the Russian, communist rule, which would last for the next 45 years. This will mean repudiation of the idea of ownership and no freedom of expression. Life was going to change once again for every surviving Pole. We had to leave Warsaw and we moved to a town called

My mother's English tea, Warsaw 1937

The carnage of the war

The war is over (right)

Bydgoszcz. By then I had a little sister born in the last year of war
but I have no recollection of her till she was big enough to play
with. My uncle with his family also moved to Bydgoszcz and I got
to know my cousins. The newly formed Institute of Agriculture and
Technology needed good leadership and my father and his brother
became its directors creating a first class research institution. We
were very lucky to find accommodation in a splendid villa opposite
the institute. Before the war the house belonged to an old lady who,
after the war, was allowed to have a small part of her house, the rest
was taken over by the city and let out to tenants. The new law in
the socialist system was that a person was allowed three square
metres of living space. Our new flat, the ground floor of the villa
had more space than we were allowed to have by the new rule of
law. We were allocated a man to live in the flat. This was a very
unusual man, a writer and philosopher, Jan Stachniuk. When he was
not typing his books, he worked in the institute as an odd job man.
Jan and my father had the same philosophy of life. The many discussions took place about understanding of human existence as a
dynamic and creative force. Unfortunately the new socialist system
in Poland did not allow any freedom of expression and patriotic
thought. Stachniuk's writings were discovered and he was impris-
oned, tortured and when eventually released, he was a broken man
without the ability to function normally. Although I was very
young, Stachniuk made a lasting impression on me as a dynamic,

*My family on the beach with
Jan Stachniuk (above)*

*My sister (age 6) and me
(aged 10) in Bydgoszcz (right)*

energetic and charming individual. People like him were needed in Poland where so many thinking and positive people lost their lives during the war and were executed by the Germans. Some people hoped that some sort of freedom might be established and formed new political parties. My father a positive man and great patriot, became a member of parliament representing a new party which it soon became obvious had no future in the present system. He was warned in time to get out of politics before, inevitably he would end up in prison. I went to Warsaw with him to listen to the speech he made in the parliament. He talked about the need of creating a new

man in Poland whose leading motto should be "my worth is in what I created". Although I was young and most probably did not follow the meaning of his speech, the importance of the occasion imprinted itself on my memory. I think that he managed to avoid arrest because as a food specialist and a scientist he was needed in the new socialist reality but he made a wise decision and left politics in 1952.

Family in Bydgoszcz

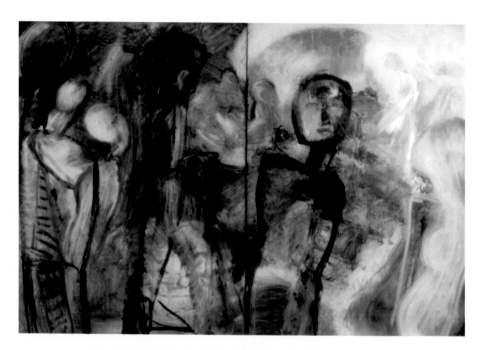

The Journey – *oil on board, 1985*

I was eight years old when for the first time I had to go to school. I disliked it intensely. The long walk along dull fields, carrying a heavy briefcase sitting at a desk in the class with lots of strangers was a miserable experience. I was always the tallest in the class and for that reason was laughed at and called names. The best part of the day was when I was free after school to go across the road to the institute and play in the vast fields, hedges, trees and orchards. There was a group of us, all children of the people working there. We had a great time playing hide and seek and making dens in bushes. Crawling under enormous rhubarb plants was a special fun. In the summer when the days were very sunny, my mother kept us away from school and took us for walks in the nearby woods or made us sit on our terrace and read. She insisted that it was much healthier for us than sitting in the class room. In the hall of our flat stood a grand piano which belonged to the owner but was left downstairs and we could use it. Both my parents played well, it was part of their education. Sometimes my parents would play something they still remembered and I loved the sound of it. My mother refused my wish to learn on the grounds that it requires hours of practice which would not be a healthy thing to do. However since I wanted to play, she bought a mandolin and I managed to play a few tunes before losing interest. Reading I loved but drawing even more so. I needed paper for drawing, not always available in shops but I had an idea which has caused my first physical punishment. I picked up a big volume from the bookshelf and tore out the blank sheet – a fly leaf. It was very smooth and brilliant white, a joy to draw on. Unfortunately my father did not agree with me, it was an expensive book *Das Kapital* by Karl Marx. For the first time, I was punished and it hurt! I was growing very fast and became anaemic with many nosebleeds which made me miserable. The sport sessions at school were exhausting me and a decision was taken to take me out of school for a long rest in the country. I was sent to a forester's house which was a small farm with a horse and a few cows. The countryside was beautiful with hills and forests. There were tall

Madre Mia – *oil on board, 1981*

hollyhocks and sunflowers everywhere. Semi-wild cats were breeding freely and I had fun trying to catch the kittens. The cows were taken every morning to a distant field and one day, the forester suggested that perhaps I would enjoy taking them there. That was when I have learned that they are rather stupid animals who would wander all over the woods instead of staying on the path. Each cow went in different direction. I had to chase them through the undergrowth of nettles and by the time we reached the required destination, I was exhausted and made sure that I will not have to repeat that activity. Apart from helping with varied tasks on the farm, I had to rest. A deckchair was placed on a hillside and I was wrapped up in a blanket reading and resting. The valley spreading in front of me with constantly changing light, the vibrant nature, the silence of the nearby forest became a cherished memory. I returned home much healthier. Missing 40 days of the dreaded school did not bother me in the least.

My mother was deeply affected by the war, she suffered from debilitating headaches and depressions. She was hospitalised for long periods and given draconian treatment. My sister and I were kept in the dark about my mother's illness and our life was continuing almost as normal because our beloved grandmother came to look after us. I remember that time especially because she took me with her to the big farmer's market to buy, among other things, chickens. Once a live bird had to be killed in the kitchen and my grandmother did not wish me to be present to witness the procedure. However, I walked in just after the head was cut off and saw the headless body running around. It made me very upset and it took a long time before I was willing to eat chicken again. My grandmother was very kind and loving and whenever it was possible, she liked to indulge her granddaughters. She loved having a small cup of the espresso coffee and one day she allowed me to taste it. I remember the delicious sweet taste of it. These secret indulgences made me feel grown up.

Every weekend, in the summer time, my father took us to the river and rowed us in an old wooden boat. Rowing was my father's great passion and since his youth he won many races in Poland and abroad. In the thirties he was a national champion in the skulls. Summertime was the rowing time and we always walked on a Sunday morning towards the river while the majority of the population, dressed in the Sunday best, walked towards the church. My mother was a devout Catholic, while my father was an agnostic. She was very accommodating and accepted the shortcomings of the church as an institution, while my father was very critical of it. My first communion was almost a secret affair and the very first confession took place while I was sick and in bed. The priest's visit was somehow sensed by my father and made him very annoyed. This was the first row that I witnessed as a child and in order that we should not understand it was conducted in English. As it happened this first communion was a terrible experience for me. In fact I never received it because the priest missed me out. I was the last girl standing at the altar waiting to receive it and the priest did not notice me in spite of my height. When we all returned to our seats I felt terrible shame and embarrassment. My mother obviously did not notice and I was not going to tell her. This accidental occurrence did not help my poor self-esteem and self-assurance. I was terribly shy and at that age had not got close friends. Real friendships formed much later when I was fourteen. Reading and drawing were my favourite occupations outside the school hours. At that age, I went to hear my first concert and the first opera. The concert was taking place in the town hall and on the night during the performance of Beethoven's *Eroica* a huge chandelier crashed and landed just behind the conductor and in front of the first row of the audience. It smashed all the intricate pieces of glass but the conductor and the orchestra did not stop playing till the last note.

My mother loved oriental objects and we had some beautiful translucent cups for tea and embroidered wall hangings which enriched the otherwise sparse interior. Naturally, when the opera

Madame Butterfly arrived in our town, my mother took me to see it. It was a psychological character study in beautiful costumes and romantic arias. I cried much at the end because the sadness of the story was very moving. My parents' close friends were two couples with whom they socialised. My favourite was Dr and Mrs Joncher, He was a most charming doctor who looked after our health. Whenever I was ill, he would arrive and address me: "how are you the old horse?" He had a lovely sense of humour much needed because his wife was the most eccentric person in our provincial town. The gossip columns in the daily paper always had something to say about Mrs Joanna Joncher. I remember her two little poodles always dressed in colourful jerkins. She dyed her hair in many shades of red and dressed in splendid sophisticated outfits designed by herself and made by a local dressmaker. On a particular day of the week she walked to our only acceptable cafe where she drew the attention of customers and the passers-by. Her bright lipstick was never neatly applied adding to her unorthodox style.

Money matters between her and her husband were never talked about but took place via notes which were placed in an oriental vase. The aim was to avoid any possible confrontation about such mundane issues. Their only daughter was a talented painter and one day Mrs Joanna decided to start painting also. I went to all exhibitions which took place in our town hall and it was obvious that sooner or later, an artist would paint a portrait of Mrs Joanna. She was after all a very colourful subject. The portrait of her was not complimentary and Joanna was going to do something about it. Secretly, she found a hiding place in the building and during the night she virtually repainted the offending portrait of herself. I can imagine what the gossip columns had to say about it and I wonder what the author of the portrait had to say! Her own painting were very dreamy and atmospheric and always on the subject of woman. Her daughter Barbara supported her mother's artistic endeavours. Although I attended every annual exhibition in our town, I never tried to paint a picture. I had a very good art teacher at school who

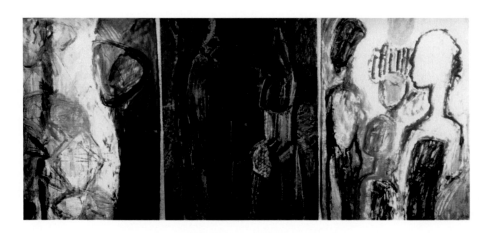

Triptych 2 – *on paper, 1996*

encouraged experimentation with colours and drawing. One particular experiment was using hot wax which we applied to a
handkerchief and then scrunched it. Afterwards it was dipped in a
dye. It gave a rich texture which for me was an eye-opener. There
was more to art than reproducing the world around, the things we
see. One could achieve something new using different tools to create textures. A seed of discovery had been planted and making art
became for me the most pleasurable activity. Every Christmas and
Easter time, my mother asked me to make cards which she sent to
relatives and special friends. I had to produce 15 individual cards.
Both my parents supported me and encouraged me in my artistic
efforts and it gave me great pleasure. The only person in our family
who was completely unable to express approval or praise was my
father's mother – grandma Makey. She was highly critical of everything and everybody. Later on in life when I learned about psychology I began to understand why my father, and his brother and
sister, almost never hugged or embraced members of family. This
must have been due to the conditioning that they received during
their disciplined, emotionally deprived childhood. There was not
much love or joy in their family. I was afraid of that grandmother
and tried to avoid her when she happened to visit us which, luckily,
was not often. I was, however curious about her very rotund body
and I wanted to see her without the flowing garments. This was
possible while she was going to have a bath when I was hoping to
peep through the keyhole. It wasn't to be because her big body
filled all the visible limited space which the keyhole gave me!
Children love hearing stories and she must have had a lot to tell
because she brought up five children alone when her husband
suddenly died after the First World War. He was the creator and
owner of the first Polish mail-order catalogue. All the money he
made was invested in shares and when the First World War came,
he lost all his invested money. Shortly after, he suffered a stroke
and his wife was left with five children to bring up alone. I was told
that she was selling one harmonium each month – a residue from

the catalogue collection and worked in the drugstore. I would have loved to hear her stories unfortunately it was not to be because she moved to a distant town to be with her daughter, my aunt Mira who was equally eccentric as her mother.

One day a big dog came to our household, his name was Rex and I disliked him from the start. He was supposed to assist my father in the hunting expeditions. Unfortunately Rex had other ideas and as soon as the duck was shot and he was ordered to fetch it, Rex disappeared to consume it. When he was at home, he learned how to open the front door and to wonder off returning when he was hungry. Another awful habit of his was to sit during meal time, by my chair, salivating and having a permanent erection. It was obvious that the dog had to go back to the farmer who gave him to my father. The only sad person was my sister Ika who since early childhood loved dogs and yet never throughout her long life managed to have one.

My primary school issued two certificates each year. The 13 subjects were graded and the information about the days of absence were also given. Since my health on the whole was not very good, every year, I missed many days of the dreaded school. My lowest grades were in geography, the subject with which I seemed to have problems. Perhaps the teacher was bad! If a child had many unacceptable grades she had to repeat the year. Luckily for me, it never happened and my best grade was for behaviour. I also had a good grade for singing which mystified me since I am unable to sing a single note. Once when I tried to join a choir the choirmaster dismissed me after hearing the false notes. The only reason why I wanted to join the choir was the presence of a handsome boy who sang beautifully and I wanted to meet him. It happened much later when on a lovely summer's day with a small group of friends, we decided to play truant and went to play volleyball in the nearby woods! A piece of rope, instead of a net hung between two trees and we had great time playing. This was our last summer in that school. We were all 14 years old, the time when friendships are formed and the interest in the opposite sex stirs. We were going to start secondary school and for my family a big change of moving to another city. My father was often absent, lecturing in the Technical University of Gdansk. He installed a camp bed in his department when his stay was longer than a day. This was obviously an awful arrangement and since the post of the head of the department was a permanent one we had to move to Gdansk on the Baltic Coast. It was a very exciting time and a great challenge for my father who was creating a new department of Organic Chemistry. Gdansk, Sopot and Gdynia are the three cities almost joined and yet very different. Gdansk had the famous shipyards and was a medieval city of trade, Sopot was a spa town with a magnificent pier and extensive woods and beaches while Gdynia was a fishing port which grew over the years into a residential town and large harbour for yachts. All three cities were connected by an electric train and one highway. My mother wished to find a flat in Sopot which was in her eyes the healthiest of all the three cities. As it happened, a couple wished to exchange a flat and move to Bydgoszcz. It was a fantastic good luck and a new chapter in our lives was about to begin.

2. New Beginning: Growing Up

The sea, once it casts its spell,
it holds one in its net of wonder for ever.

Jacques Cousteau

Gdansk after the war

It is 1951, I am 14 years old and we are starting a new life on the Baltic Coast. I wanted to visit and investigate the new area, above all the old medieval trading city of Gdansk. It was six years since the war ended and the city was still in ruin. I wandered between the remains of the old walls and imagined what it must have looked like in its heyday. During the following five years much was going to change in Gdansk. The old streets were being restored and the town rebuilt. The small town of Sopot was almost untouched by the war. The elegant town houses stood silent and waiting for the new occupants when the war was over. Each house, before the war was occupied by one family, now had multiple occupation. A person had the right to occupy

Academy of Art, Gdansk

three square metres. Large flats were subdivided into smaller ones. Our flat had no kitchen and a tiny bathroom created out of a utility storage space. A stove and sink was installed in the corner of a back room. This was going to be the kitchen-studio, so called by my mother. She was a genius in making our three room flat

Our first floor flat in the Sopot house

into a new delightful dwelling. The kitchen room was ingeniously turned into her language studio by using tall screens covered with blue fabric. This was the room for preparing and eating meals and for giving English lessons. It had a very big round table, covered with the same fabric as the screens. The overall colour was blue-white, very cheerful and pleasant. The other two rooms had to be organised in such a way that we could sleep, study and live in them, like the English bedsits. You had to walk through the first one to the second one so privacy of any kind was out of question. Once again, my mother created a lovely sitting room with shelves along its long wall and the two beds which fitted underneath and were pulled out for the night. A big settee was on the opposite wall with a window behind it overlooking the balcony, which was big enough to have a makeshift bed made out of packing boxes. Two folding deckchairs filled in the rest of the space. The balcony was facing south and was a wonderful sun-trap. We all sat there and sometimes a lucky person could sleep there in the summer. My parents occupied the second room which was also my father's study. The walls were lined with shelves on which stood endless files all well marked. He was the most organised person I ever met. He used to

On the doorstep of the new home in Sopot

say that you are well organised if you can find anything you need with closed eyes. The lovely antique desk with many drawers contained his tools which also hung on the hooks screwed into its side wall. If anybody wished to borrow a tool, he expected it to be put back in its right place. Father also had his own sewing box with everything needed for replacing mainly buttons on his shirts. He insisted on doing it himself. The old spools of cotton went back to the pre-war time and many needles were slightly rusted with time. It was fun to watch the professor threading the needle with much too long thread and getting it tangled up while dealing with the button. He did not mind when we laughed and was happy if one of us offered assistance.

Our rooms were heated in winter with coal which my father brought from the cellar in buckets. Before he went to work he prepared the two big old fashioned, tiled stoves which were in the corner of each of the two rooms. They looked awful, took a lot of space but for the next few years this was the only way to keep us warm.

On the floor below us, lived a policeman with his wife and two children. It worried my mother, who was sure that his presence there, below us meant that he would listen to our conversations. Many times she warned my father with words still imprinted on my memory "the walls have ears". The man, was most probably very suspicious when he heard laughter coming from the flat above his, after all nobody had reasons to laugh much in the Polish reality. Food was limited and even toilet paper was difficult to buy. People used to pop into any shop while passing by in case there was something to buy. One day, my father was very lucky when on his way from work, he went into a shop where toilet paper had just arrived. He bought as many rolls as the woman was willing to sell him and threaded them like a necklace. He walked back home showing off his find and was stopped by many people who wished to know where it came from. If you went to store to buy toilet paper most likely you will be offered sandpaper which was always available! This was one of the well-known jokes.

Across the street from our house was a short avenue leading to the forest which was the beginning of very extensive and hilly woods going on for many miles. It was such a beautiful area where I loved to wonder and feel in one with nature. A small lake sunk deep amongst the trees had fisherman sitting around it in the summertime. Further on was an open air theatre which in the summer had many lively performances of operas and pop concerts. These were amplified to the extent that the noise reached our house and kept us awake. The only animals living in those woods were the Wild Boars and almost no birds were heard in spite of the lush and unspoiled environment. Sometimes a wild boar came out of the woods to look for food. In time, people started leaving food for them and the whole family of the Wild Boars would venture out unafraid of people.

In adjacent street, once a week farmers arrived to sell their produce. This was a wonderful market. My mother had favourite women from whom she bought fresh vegetables, honey and eggs.

My parents walking in the Sopot's wood

Once I went with my uncle to the market. He was asked by my mother to buy some eggs. He walked along the row of women sitting on their little stools always wearing scarves. Having spotted the most pretty girl, he asked for the eggs from a black hen. The young woman would say that she did not know which eggs were laid by a black hen! My uncle reassured her that he certainly knew and promptly chose the biggest eggs.

I am not sure if the woman ever understood the joke but my mother was very happy with my uncle's purchase. She adored her brother Ric and her sister Zula. Unfortunately they lived in a distant Warsaw. The time of their visit was the happiest for my mother who suffered debilitating depressions and long lasting headaches. During their stay, she never had headaches and was the happiest of people. Ric and Zula were the most positive and cheerful members of our family in spite of the fact that both had bad luck in choosing partners. Uncle always fell for a "silly blond", sexy but vain who sooner or later departed leaving Uncle Ric heartbroken. The one marriage of his was a disaster and so was my aunt's. She married a man who was ruled by his mother who decided to move in with his newly married son. The two-room flat was going to spell disaster in the married life of my aunt. The mother was highly critical of everything that the new wife was doing and interfered in their everyday life. The divorce was inevitable followed by my aunt's decision to move to the small flat of her brothers. Both of them spoke many languages and for many years they gave English lessons to adults. They met some lovely people who became their friends for many years. Their teaching schedule was punishing – eight hours a day and they saved for two years after which time they went on a journey aboard a trading ship. These ships had only a few cabins for passengers and they called on many ports on the long voyages often to the Far East. Ric took photos and upon return from the voyages he invited his students for the slide show and told many interesting stories. Aunt Zula was his faithful companion although she suffered from arthritis and the long voyages were not easy for her. When they visited us in Sopot, my Aunt would sit on the sunny balcony and administered herself a fashionable cure for arthritis – a sting from a bee. I was watching her holding a small netted frame inside which a bee was trapped. She applied this poor trapped bee to her thigh and the irritated bee stung her, promptly dying. The venom injected was supposed to have healing power. My Aunt swore that it had a good effect and improved her condition. Over the following years, they took many exotic voyages and she had to be reasonably fit to cope with not exactly luxurious conditions on the boats.

The two months of our first summer holiday on the Baltic Coast were magical. Swimming in the sea, long walks in the woods, and sightseeing passed very fast. The bay along which Gdansk, Sopot and Gdynia were situated was sheltered by the peninsula called Hel behind which was the open sea. Unfortunately the long open Baltic Coast was mostly out of bounds for Poles. The beautiful beaches were ploughed and fenced except for limited areas. Tall wooden towers were erected along the coast and a poor soldier with a gun was on duty to keep an eye on any Pole who might wish to escape to Sweden. Private ownership of boats did not exist but sometimes a solitary yacht belonging to a club was seen sailing in the open sea. From time to time some brave man tried to row to the island of Bornholm, the nearest point of contact with the capitalist West. These efforts were mostly futile and ended tragically.

The small towns along the coast had an area of the beach allocated for swimming and walking under the ever watchful eye of the sentry who used binoculars to observe holidaymakers. I loved walking as far as it was allowed to pick up small pieces of amber. I imagined the time when Baltic Sea was a huge forest 30 million years ago during the Eocene Epoch. When cooling took place, turning forests into open countryside, resin flowed from the extinct trees. The Baltic Coast is rich in amber deposits and the stormy sea throws small amounts onto the sandy beaches. Amber was highly prized by sun-worshipping peoples, such as Phoenicians, the Romans and the Greeks. It has been used as a talisman against sickness and bad luck, and as a cure for many illnesses. It is still used as a healing stone by some people. There are over 200 different shades and colours of amber from almost white to dark brown and blue. They are especially precious when they contain fossilised remains of plants and animals, beautifully preserved. The value of such specimens can reach thousands of pounds.

When my father bought a small sailing boat we were able to motor from Gdansk through many canals to the estuary cut off from the sea - 4 km wide and 20 km long. The strip of land separating these

On father's sailing boat, Strybog

waters, from the Baltic Sea was wooded and magnificently isolated. A few yachts which sailed on the Zalew belonged to the sailing clubs and were mostly used by the students. Some of them knew my father and wrote satirical articles in the university magazine about the encounters with the professor who sailed in a small boat lined with the wild boar skins. The boat was called *Strybog* – the pagan god of winds. The expeditions with my father took usually a few weeks and were always full of unexpected adventures. I had to be brave and very, very tidy. The discipline which "the Captain" imposed was hard but useful, in my later life. We encountered sudden storms as well as blissfully serene weather conditions with gentle winds and lots of sun. The shores of the estuary were mostly wild with dense forests. One of the special places where we moored the boat was a small sleepy town Frombork. The town was famous because Copernicus lived there and made his famous observations. His observation tower was damaged by the shelling during the war. Every time we came to Frombork I went up the damaged tower and sat on the top imagining what it must have looked like when the great astronomer gazed at the sky. There was such a spiritual charge in that deserted and neglected place. I wondered what Copernicus life was like when he made such monumental discoveries and was deprived of a chance to publish it. Excommunication would have

Sun worshipers
– my uncle with my
father on Strybog

been inevitable should his theory became the public knowledge. A young German astronomer came to visit him and took with him the manuscript back to Germany to have it printed. When it was done, he returned to Copernicus who by then was dying. His life's work in the great book was placed on the bed of the dying man who could depart in the knowledge that the result of his scientific discovery was not done in vain.

Along the opposite shore, the northern side of Zalew a long strip of hilly and wooded land was separating it from the open Baltic Sea. Only at some points, one could get down to the beach but mostly, the barbed wire fencing kept people firmly away. When *Strybog* moored in some wild spot of the northern shore of Zalew, it was a special time to roam through the wilds of the forest. This area of the coast was a scene of heavy fighting during the war. The remains of deep trenches now filled with vegetation were everywhere and while wandering there, I picked all sorts of objects. The buttons from the uniforms of the German soldiers were the most common find. Mushrooms grew on the sandy soil and I often came back to *Strybog* with handfuls of aromatic Bolitos. Wonderful supper was then prepared by my father cooked on a pocket size collapsible cooker. Most of the time, I was a hungry while Captain was quite satisfied with minimal quantities of food. Returning home, after weeks of sailing and having had no access to a mirror, I could hardly recognise myself. My face was thin and very brown while the hair was bleached by the sun.

Every sailing holiday was always connected with some dangerous moments. Once we were in the middle of the Zalew Estuary when a very sudden storm overwhelmed our small boat. It was necessary to take down the small sail called a jib. This required from me bravery. I had to get to the very front of the boat, unshackle the jib and remove it while the boat was being tossed mercilessly by the very strong wind. When the ordeal was over, my father praised my bravery in following his orders and avoiding falling overboard. We were exhausted by the storm and relentless rain. That night, we were going to sleep on the smelly, drenched skins of the wild boars! Sometimes, my father tried my bravery to its limits. One particular evening, when we moored on the Vistula River on the return journey from Zalew, Captain asked me to clamber a steep wooded shore and go to a farm where, he hoped, we could buy some milk. It wouldn't have been beyond my capability except that I could hear very angry dogs barking in the distant. Most farmers kept dogs on long chains in the yards. I hoped that this time I was going to be safe and climbed up the steep slope full of nettles and brambles.

The farmer was amazed to see suddenly a tall woman approaching from nowhere. The dogs went crazy but the chains were strong! Perhaps, he thought that I was some sort of apparition. My can was filled with rich creamy milk for which he did not charged me anything. Going back to the boat, down the wet slope was much worse than going up. It was getting dark and the drizzly rain made it all much worst. Now days, when I buy a tin of powdered milk, I think how much easier it would have been to have such luxury on the boat. Our *Strybog* had a most primitive little engine, the only one available at the time.

It was unreliable piece of equipment giving us constant trouble. It was necessary to use it while navigating through canals from Gdansk to Zalew and back when sailing was impossible. If we were lucky and a Russian barge on its way to Gdansk obliged and allowed us to attach our boat to its side, we were moving at a fair speed. These barges were empty coming to Poland and very heavy and submerged on the way out. They had no understanding of how damaging to the shore line they were, travelling at high speed with heavy loads along the narrow rivers and canals. The huge wave behind them was constantly eroding the shore line and all the vegetation. Every year, the shore line was widening and more subsidence visible.

The holidays of two months over, I was ready to start the new school – Technical Art College, till the age of nineteen when I will go to the higher education. I had to acquire the reasonable knowledge in 25 subjects. My college was a fair distance from our house and I had to take a train to get to school for the start at 8 am and finish at 3 pm, including Saturdays. We had extra activities, which included army training and work at the farming cooperative. We

Sculpting at school

slept on straw in the barns and worked the whole day in the field, usually picking potatoes and filling the sacks. Each year we also had to plant forests, the activity that had a special meaning for me and which I loved. Somewhere on the Baltic Coast a row of pines

which I planted must now be fully grown. For a young person all these activities were very agreeable as well as fun.

My favourite teacher was a tall, handsome always well-dressed man whose speech was clear and manner elegant. His name was the equivalent of the word in English – reindeer.

He taught us the history of art with great preference for the Greek art and architecture. We had few visual aids and the books were poorly printed with black and white reproductions and yet he instilled in us the interest in the history of the past cultures, the temples of Parthenon, the decorated pots and magnificent sculptures.

Head of Bozena, college work

The lessons were full of legends, mythology and the old tales. We remembered for many years all that he told us and had highest grades in his subject.

Apart from the usual academic subjects, we had art which included sculpture, painting, design and, very important, the technology of art. My favourite one was painting and drawing. Our teacher was an artist who had definite views about many things and seem to know what was real art and what was so called "kitsch". He did not tolerate colours pink and black – insisting that the first one is for underwear and the second, a negation of colour. One day, we were given a project of painting or drawing a portrait. I loved children and I drew with pastels a portrait of a young child. My parents thought that it was a lovely piece of work and I went to school anticipating the teacher's approval. All the work produced by our class was placed on the floor for the teacher's viewing. Somehow, he pointed first of all at my work and I quickly realised that something was not right. In fact he dismissed it as an awful work and warned me that if I continue producing such "kitsch" again, I will have to leave his class.

Study in 3D, college work

I was so humiliated that it took me a long time to get over it. My ever supportive parents helped me to get back the self-assurance and I did not give up. The following year I won a drawing competition for an interpretation of statues on display in the Museum of Gdansk.

My dislike of the teacher never left me and I considered the incident to be a valuable lesson of what not to do in a teaching situation. Since that time I mistrust all art teachers who so often impose their views and are unnecessarily critical, leaving no room for a dialogue with the student. Our art studios were situated almost on the beach which meant that in the summer after school, I could take a long walk home along the shore. I loved the sea, its ever changing light on the glistening surface, the sound of the waves and the patterns they left on the sandy shore. I wished the school time could go on for many more years but, as time goes on and the end was near, I had to think what I wanted to do next.

A the end of my studies, I received a diploma of the Technic of Plastic Arts. I was nineteen and ready for the next stage of my education.

Astronomy interested me greatly since the time when, I had an unexpected chance to join a group of enthusiastic young people who had telescopes. I saw for the first time the moon surface and the sky full of stars. I have learned about different constellations and the distant planets. It had a dramatic impact on my imagination. Apart from the realisation of the minuteness of our planet in the universe it was our existence on it which seem like a miracle. These observations to my young mind connected with the concept of Time. The awareness of the very limited time in comparison to the eternal time of space opened new horizons to me. Once I became aware of the concept of Time other thoughts followed. How am I going to use that time allocated to me? Is art a useful thing to humanity? Who actually needs my art? Isn't there all around me enough art? Should I not contribute something more useful to humanity? I went a few times to my father's department to take part in some organoleptic assessment of food products. This is a fascinating field of

Human Predicament, *mixed technique on paper*

organic chemistry dealing with food technology. So much more useful to human existence than art. It interested me every time I joined his department in some testing and appraisal of food samples. This was a pioneering research. The more I thought about it the more I felt optimistic about following in his footsteps. Once I discussed it with my ever-supportive parents, I had to prepare myself for the entrance exam which was purely academic with chemistry and maths, the two subjects in which I was very poor. If I wanted to become an organic chemist, I was willing to have tutorials which would enable me to pass the entrance exam. I passed it and the family was delighted. The bewildering and intense first year of studies began but it wasn't long before the thought dawned on me that I have made a mistake. I missed the art, the freedom of experimentation and the challenge of totally different kind. The demands of the science subjects were too much for me and I had to return to doing what I liked most. Perhaps my parents knew that I was not made for science but were wise to support my plan and let me try the sciences.

While I was at the university I joined the volleyball team and met some lovely women from different walks of life. We had trainings twice a week and played many games. One particular game was going to be played in Ostrava a town in Czechoslovakia. It took a lot of persuading before my mother agreed for me to take part in it.

I was immensely looking forward to my first trip abroad. Ostrava is an industrial city south of Poland, on the other side of the Tatra Mountains. The trip by overnight train left our team exhausted. We were met by the welcoming team and served a huge meal. We had one training on that day, followed by sleep in an old school classroom. The next morning after a big breakfast with most delicious cakes, ham, cheeses, etc. we were in poor condition to play the first match. We ate too much and our readiness for the game was going to suffer. We had to change in the sports hall into the proper kit and while I put my hand into my bag I experienced a sharp pain in the tips of my fingers. The razor blades were scattered in my bag! What horror!! My fingers had to be covered with plasters to stop bleeding but, in spite of the pain, I was determined to play. My strongest points were the serving during which I managed to avoid using the cut fingertips. We never discovered how a packet of razor blades got into my bag or why. The most important thing was that we won this game and went home singing. While we were in Ostrava, we had an hour free to walk around the nearest shops. This was our first trip outside of Poland and everything around us was interesting and different. The shops were as poor as ours but objects in them looked different. I was particularly enchanted by a little black doll. We never saw coloured people in Poland and this doll was most unusual, I loved her. I cannot remember having dolls as a child. According to a portrait of me as a three-year-old child, I must have had a doll because there is one sitting next to me. I am sure that everybody thought me rather odd, buying a doll at my age. From the moment I got her, she became my mascot, a little doll with smiling face! When Christmas time came, I wanted to buy little gifts for my parents and my sister Ika. I had no money but I knew that I could sell this precious doll.

With heavy heart, I took her to the second hand stall in our covered market and the woman gave me good money seeing such an unusual doll. The following day, my mother noticed the absence of my precious mascot and having sensed how upset I was, she insisted that I get her back. I never did, such unusual doll was very easy to sell and it went to another home, before I managed to come back for her.

My volleyball team

My parents differed greatly in the approach to our upbringing. My father believed in facing tough challenges and learning to deal with them while my mother constantly worried about our safety.

For example, it was difficult to persuade her to allow us to take part in outings organised by the school. When and if she agreed, I knew that she would worry till our safe return. I never told her about the accident which I had on one such outing. We were going to ski in the Tatra Mountains for a few days and I was looking forward to this adventure. My skiing experience was limited to cross country only and I never went down the hill. It was going to be something new and like all my friends, I was very excited. On the very first day of our arrival in the spectacular snowy mountains, we were told to put the skis on and ski down an unknown to us slope which looked rather bumpy. This is the only pleasure I had, the joy of going very fast down that hill. The next thing I will always remember was waking up and seeing lots of laughing faces leaning over me. I just came back from the most beautiful world of music. I was rocked by great swans to that sound of heavenly music. I did not like the greyness of the world which was around me and wished to return to the other one. I lost memory for a while because coming down that lovely hill I was unable to stop, fell and hit a rock. How the rock encountered my head, I will never know! Our teacher was relieved that after 35 hours I regained consciousness and she avoided having to call medical help. She was obviously not a very intelligent teacher. My headache was horrendous and it took some time before I remembered who I was. The details of my life were coming back like turning pages of a book which was full of lovely stories. My parents never learned about my accident. I often wondered about the experience of the "other" world which was so beautiful. Perhaps this will be the beginning of a journey after I die! The accident made me look at the world and my existence differently. Life can end suddenly and unexpectedly, but perhaps we do not have to worry about it, and it might be that there is another dimension into which we shall journey. My inner life has been enriched by an accident which could have been fatal but luckily was not.

Another adventure was awaiting me, the following summer, this time a very pleasant one. On the same floor in our house, lived a family whose daughter was an archaeologist and spent a lot of her time working on some ancient excavations. She needed somebody who could draw and was interested in taking part in the next project. I was delighted when my mother agreed that I could join Jola to a very distant village somewhere in the middle of Poland. The countryside was very flat with never-ending fields crisscrossed with rushing streams. Summers in Poland are usually very hot and there was no shelter from the sun at the excavations site. My work consisted of drawing plans of the different layers which were being excavated. At lunch break I ran to a stream, stripped naked and wallowed in the cooling water. In the evenings we spent hours reviewing our finds – usually pieces of pottery and metal. Intelligent group of archaeologists always had interesting stories to share. This was a very pleasing holiday activity.

Jola's mother was an excellent cook and was willing to teach me and my sister to make some interesting dishes using the very limited products available. My mother kept us away from the kitchen/studio because she was of the opinion that we would have to learn how to cook when the time came and we had our own families. While we were young, we should do more interesting things. She disliked cooking but, always produced beautifully presented meals. The early supper was our main meal of the day. My father always admired the presentation of the dish saying that the eyes ought to feast first before the taste buds were engaged. My mother was a perfectionist in everything she did. She loved teaching and her lessons were always full of laughter. Her students loved her sense of humour and encouragement. She created her own unique method of teaching and her students were never bored. In spite of a very limited choice of clothing in the shops, she always knew how to put together pieces which would look stylish and were admired especially by my father who was exceptional amongst majority of men in noticing what women wore. Both my parents cared about the way they looked and they instilled this in both of their daughters. I remember the time when my father wanted to give me a present of a dress. I was very tall and there was nothing available in the few shops around. But, he suggested that I could buy a fabric and have a frock made by a dressmaker. I found a lilac colour, very woolly fabric and it was made into a dress which was narrow at the hem and looked like a sack. Such was the fashion at that time. I was delighted but quickly discovered two major problems. The fabric was itchy like hell and the narrowness at the hem did not allow me to walk up the stairs. The only way I could ascend was sideways!

The time came when my mother's health deteriorated and she needed help with every day chores. This was when Mrs Gertruda was employed in spite of my father's dislike of the presence of a stranger. She loved us from the very start but was aware that my father disapproved of her presence. He believed that a person has to be self-sufficient. Some men hate admitting that they need help as I discovered many times in the future years. In the eyes of my father it was the admission of weakness. After many weeks, he could see how much such help improved my mother's wellbeing and accepted Mrs Gertruda. She, however, never quite felt happy when he was around.

In the kitchen-studio, in one corner stood a big trunk, the kind with which well to do passengers travelled on the ocean liners. It was my mother's trunk with which she returned from her years of work in the twenties in Chicago. We did not take much notice of it until the day when a space was needed for a refrigerator which was bought with enormous difficulty. The only space for it was where the trunk stood. This was the moment of great surprise for us, two teenage girls. My sister and I were completely in awe when my mother opened the trunk. The whole interior was lined with soft brilliant green fabric and one side of it had many drawers while the other had a curtain behind which hang coat hangers with some lovely silky garments. In the drawers were some elegant ladies shoes and other strange looking beauty accessories. I suspect that the trunk survived the war hidden in a home of two old spinster aunts who lived in a small provincial town. We both loved this magic moment of entering the world of the bygone days and I suspect that my mother could have told us some interesting stories from the time of her work for years in the USA. Both my parents were reluctant about reminiscing, perhaps it was painful for them. The world lost to the war!

In California lived Prof. Hodgson whose wife, Evelin, was the kindest of people, always ready to help. They met my father when he was in Berkley before the war working in the same field of food technology as Evelin's husband. They became friends and I always addressed her as Aunt Evelin. After the war, she sent us parcels with second hand clothes knowing that our tall family was going to have never-ending problems. Whenever a parcel arrived it was like a Christmas time. There was always something for each member of the family and even my father delighted in a suit or jacket which

Triptych 1 – *on paper*

most probably was worn before by Prof. Hodgson who happened to be the same height. My mother meticulously removed or covered up all the labels inside the garments, especially coats to prevent them from being stolen while left hanging in some place of work or study. My trench coat from the USA was one such item, I wore it for the next ten years.

Having left the university I rejoined the art world – the Academy of Art in Gdansk situated in the medieval armoury building. The lofty halls were divided into different studios and an exhibition space. My old friends from the college were now one year ahead of me and I made new friends. These friendships were all very important and lasting. Two of my new friends were very special.

Bozena was a beautiful redhead who after her studies went to Paris and excelled in the world of fashion. My other friend Aniela became a well-known stained glass artist and for many years she taught art at the university, in the department of architecture.

Completely different group of friends were the volleyball players. Krystyna and Stefan are my lifelong friends from the team group.

My time at the Academy was very constructive, all our lecturers were practising artists who helped us to develop our own individual interests. There was no imposition of personal views or theories, questioning and dialogue was the method our teachers used. I particularly liked the three-dimensional sculptural sessions in which the study of form and texture were more challenging. I wish I had more time for experimentation in that medium. Some very famous artists came as visiting lecturers, but I missed meeting them and the only contact I made was through the publications that kind friends have send to me.

Life is a process of constant change and in unexpected circumstances can suddenly change everything. It happened to me in 1958 as a result of my birth in the Warsaw's clinic in 1937.

3. London

Trust your intuition, it rarely deceives you, act on it and with a whole heart do what you are meant to do.

Geza Vermes

The two girls born at the same time in Warsaw in 1937 met different fates. Much of their survival during the war was due to luck. My parents, my sister, who was born in the middle of the war, and I were lucky, we survived but lost everything. The mother of the other little girl, Maria, was taken to Russia during the war as were many women and their children. The terrible winter and hunger caused deaths of many women and children. Maria survived but her little baby died of cold and the lack of food. Maria was on that journey until she reached England and was reunited with her husband Tadeusz. She was a deeply religious person. Prayer and hope kept her alive throughout the traumatic exodus. She was never to see her country again and she did not know where, on the Russian soil, her baby is buried.

The largest concentration of Poles was in England where they formed an army and the famous Polish Air Squadrons. Poles hoped to return to the free country after the war. The Yalta Agreement between Stalin, Roosevelt and Churchill destroyed

Me with Tadeusz and Maria Zawidzki on the balcony of their house in South Kensington

that hope. Poland was going to become part of the Russian empire. It must have been a shocking reality for the thousands of Poles who fought for their country in vain. Maria and Tadeusz had to start a new life in London. They settled in South Kensington in a tall elegant building which, divided into bedsits, gave them income. In time, they learned that our family survived the war and wished very much to invite me to visit them in order to see what their daughter would have looked like had she not died. Getting a passport and permission for travel to the West was an enormous problem. My college had to agree first of all after which an official letter with invitation from London had to be submitted to the appropriate offices to obtain visa and the passport. My mother was determined to achieve her goal while my father was rather doubtful. He was not certain as to my ability to cope away from family's protective care. After months of waiting, visa and passport arrived and the ticket for the boat had to be paid for. My mother borrowed the princely sum from one of her students and I was told that on the tenth of September – the day of my birthday – I will be boarding the ship, the famous *Batory* regularly making voyages between Gdynia and the USA, stopping at Tilbury. There was a great anticipation of an adventure of a lifetime.

My parents wanted to give me the opportunity which they had before the war. Their work in the USA was of great importance in their personal growth. The big difference was that I was a student and not a professional person and my knowledge of English language was limited to the written word only. Until now I had led a sheltered life within the family, looked after and supported and now, for the first time, I would have to rely on my own ability to deal with life's predicaments. Father's advice was *"You must not worry, problems always exist, imagine how boring life would be without them. Avoid depressing people, enjoy the work experience and treasure the happy moments."*

My wonderful mother was hiding the inevitable sadness at the thought of losing her older daughter in spite of believing in me and my ability to achieve some knowledge of a different culture which in her eyes was very sophisticated.

I embarked the *Batory* with much too much luggage, which I left it in the tiny cabin and rushed on the deck to have the last look at my dear family, all lined up down below, waving to me. In the dining room, through which I had to go, the tables were all set for lunch and the big bowls with exotic fruit stood on each one. Without hesitation I took a couple of oranges and, being a good thrower, aimed them at my family.

My cousin Wicek who accompanied my mother, caught both. My last link with my family and suddenly great sadness overwhelmed me, I was in tears and I did not want to go away. I will miss the warmth and the safety of my family while ahead of me was the land full of the unknown, full of strangers! My second thought was about my age. I was 21 on that day, perhaps it was the right time to try my independence and see the different world. After all I will be returning after a while and everything will be back to normal again. The boat moved away from the key but I stood on the deck till the Polish shore disappeared. My thoughts were with my mother who, I knew would return home starting her awful headache, crying much, while I will be far at sea with trepidation looking forward to the adventure of my life.

In the ship's dining room, we were allocated a table and a place for the duration of our journey. Two couples were at my table, Mr and Mrs Moss and Mr and Mrs Lukaszewich. Both couples were friendly and talkative and quickly realised that I had no experience of the world outside my country. They had a giggle seeing me trying to eat a banana without peeling it. After all I had never seen a banana before! We had, sometimes an orange thanks to a gift from my mother's pupil who happened to be a sailor's wife and whose husband often brought home some exotic fruits. So lesson no. 1 was: *how to eat a banana!* I showered the two couples with endless questions about London and by the time we docked in Tilbury I was feeling a little bit happier. The couple who invited me to England were waiting upon my arrival and I introduced to them my new friends from the voyage. In the following months I kept in contact with them visited their very different homes and was told that if ever I needed help or advice I should not hesitate to contact them.

Mr and Mrs Zawicki, the couple who invited me to London must have been very surprised when I stepped from the boat because both of them were very small as their daughter would have been, while I was 1 m 80 cm. tall and they had to look up to see my face.

It did not take me long to realise that people were free to express their thoughts and free to live the way they wished. An individual person could make decisions about their life! I knew that with freedom comes responsibility and I was not going to disappoint my hosts or my trusting parents. This trip was going to be a great learning experience. The world I came from was ruled by the system set up by the communist party depriving people of freedom of every kind. This new feeling of being overwhelmed by everything around would stay with me for a long time. So much NEW!

With Mrs Lukaszewich, 1957

I wanted to see as much as possible and experience the novelty of it all. Soon after my arrival, Mr Tadeusz drove me in his smart car to the centre of London, Oxford Circus. It was an early evening in September and it was called *a rush-hour time!* All the shop windows and the street lights were ablaze and it looked like a million of people were on the move in all directions. I was given a street map by Mr Tadeusz and told to find my way home to South Kensington. What a predicament! I stood transfixed for a long time taking in this new world. I had to *"navigate"* my way home where I knew that a nice meal prepared by

With Colonel and Mrs Moss
on another sightseeing tour

Mrs Maria awaited me. It must have been a long and slow walk back since I knew nothing about the seemingly endless buses going in all directions. It was such fun to see people popping on and off buses and a conductor standing at the entrance up the step of each bus. What a clever idea and how convenient for the passengers.

My next discovery was the amount of space people had to live in. Every adult had their own room. Did they know how lucky they were? Family houses had little gardens often in the front but mostly at the back. There were rooms to sleep in and to sit in – the sitting rooms. The bathrooms were always the coldest places where if you wished to have warm water you had to feed a strange little meter with 5p coins. You needed a few of these to get enough water for a shower.

The big town house 86 Onslow Gardens, of Maria and Tadeusz was divided into bedsits on each of the three floors. They were renting the many rooms and lived from the income generated. Their life followed a very systematic pattern – at 6 pm, they always watched the ITV news the main meal was at 3 pm. Television was a complete novelty for me.

The uncensored news and many interesting documentaries as well as the light entertainment programmes with endless laughter and fun filled their evenings.

Polish society of immigrants socialised in their famous Polish Heart Club in Kensington. Those who lived in the area usually went on Sunday to the Mass at the Brompton Oratory and afterwards to lunch at the club. I met there many members of the Polish Government in exile, generals and their wives, people with great charm and politeness, the old generation of my parents. London, the city I would fall in love with, astonished me by its richness of historical monuments, archaeological remains, museums and galleries. In the British Museum I saw the sculptures from the Parthenon and I recalled my teacher of the History of Art who with such constant enthusiasm talked about Greek temples, the goddess Athena and all that was happening 2,500 years ago. I knew that it would take a lot of time to see even a fraction of the wonderful heritage of London's rich culture and I was determined to learn first of all the spoken English language. Zawickis had a plan!

Mrs Maria suggested that I could share one of the bedsits with a charming English woman whose name was Jean. She agreed and had her rent reduced on proviso that she will help me with the everyday English language. I liked Jean very much and every morning I watched her getting ready for a secretarial job. Her clothes were lovely and her underwear even more so, I never thought that such sophisticated and delicate pieces of clothing existed. The sheer stockings which were somehow made together with the underpants and were called tights. I tried hard never to show her my awfully ugly coarse underwear although I knew that Jean would not laugh at me. She spent a long time every morning putting on very complex make up.

Her eyeshadow was deep blue, and the fine layer of fluid covered her perfect skin with a settled pink. By the time she was ready to leave for work, she looked like a film star. Jean was extremely helpful, correcting my English constantly. This was my first meeting with an English girl, and I was enchanted. Avoiding the company of Poles to speak English as much as possible was my priority. My first weeks in London were so full of unexpected experiences

and encounters which were bewildering. I was missing my volleyball games and training but I was sure to find it amongst the Polish
community. I was very fit and wished to stay that way in order not
to disappoint my team in Gdansk when I returned home. Meanwhile, I ran every evening round the Kensington area and often got
lost because all houses were the same, all painted white and of the
same style. I was learning about the famous English sense of humour when I approached a stranger, all breathless, with an inquiry
about my whereabouts! Jean was always full of laughter, when I
related my daily adventures to her. The idiomatic phrases were a
whole separate subject yet to get acquainted with. In time, I met her
boyfriend who visited her on some evenings. I understood that they
wished to be left alone and I had to go out for a few hours. The
nearby cinema the Curson, was my favourite destination where I
saw many films never available in Poland. The famous film *Gone
with the Wind* I saw at that cinema at least four times! The
American language was altogether different and I did not like the
sound of it but viewing the film a few times imprinted on my mind
some of the slang's expressions.

When I was invited by Mr and Mrs Moss, the couple I met on
the boat I knew that another world was to be discovered. They took
me out for a sightseeing tour in their big, old and elegant car. This
was my first excursion to the countryside. I was falling in love with
everything around me, the little villages, the country lanes, the
perfect gardens and the old pubs which did not exist in Poland. The
countryside looked like a huge garden and to my surprise, there
were no forests which are so much a part of the Polish countryside.
There were many signs *"Private"* indicating no access which I have
never seen in my country where private ownership did not exist
under the communist rule.

The other couple met on *Batory* – Mr and Mrs Lukaszewicz
invited me for a day to visit Kew Gardens and Richmond Park. So
much beauty! – I was filled with delight. On the walk in Richmond
Park, I picked lots of horse chestnuts to make necklaces which went

Designing with tweed and chestnut necklace

well with my coarse tweedy, woolly clothes. I was complimented on the originality of the idea. The old trees in the parks inspired me to do some drawings which met with approval and I even sold one to a charming man, Mr Nichols, who had an important position at the Home Office. That contact was extremely useful at a later stage when I needed an extension of my visa which would allow me to stay longer in England. Polish authorities were very strict and permission to extend the stay was only given on condition that it was for studies and even then it had to be the subject which did not exist at the time in Poland. To obtain such extension required a visit to the consulate offices.

This was inevitably a very unpleasant experience of having to face the most unfriendly and suspicious official. The man who interviewed me was more or less interrogating me. He wanted to know, above all, who my acquaintances were. He soon gave up the questioning because my answers were not what he expected and I was not cooperating.

I made a decision to study something related

Designing and painting for clothes— batik blouse

to the art subject but what? Again, lots of suggestions from well meaning, knowledgeable friends. It seems that Fashion Design was not a subject which one could find in Poland and it looked like a sensible choice.

I knew absolutely nothing about it and clothes did not interest me. But the thought struck me that perhaps it will be a challenge and using my art experience, I could connect the two and enjoy learning about it. It certainly would be useful knowledge. I went to St Martin's School of Art where the subject was taught and discovered that with my passed knowledge of art, I could complete the three year course in two years. It would be easier to finance the two instead of three years.

Sewing would be the most boring part of the course as I knew only how to saw a button on! The design part would be the most interesting. The college accepted me and I needed to find some money for my studies.

I was advised to visit the education department in the Ministry of Education to inquire about a possible grant. I knew that the immigrants and those Poles who had families in England were eligible for the state grant. A charming official, Mr Niedenthal who was in charge of the Education for Poles Department at the ministry informed me that regretfully, I was not eligible because I had no relatives in the UK. I had to work out the cost of my studies plus lodging, transport and food. I had faith in providential accidents and so it was that my father had an invitation to attend an international congress followed by the Rockefeller Foundation Scholarship in the USA. He was able to save enough money to cover my basic expenses during my two years of studies. On his return journey from the States, he stopped in London and I witnessed a very emotional reunion between my father and Mr Zawicki. They had seen each other last in 1937, when their daughters were born in the Warsaw clinic. For me it was also a very moving time and I realised how much I missed my family. This chance for me to obtain a diploma in Design in two years' time was going to be an achievement which would make my parents proud but it meant that I will not see them for a very long time. I was not sure how I can cope emotionally with such long separation from my family.

I was picking up the English language through reading, listening and talking and slowly, I was getting better. The incredibly polite English people went always out of their way to understand me and unfortunately, very often, couldn't be bothered to correct me.

Before my term at St Martins started I had to find a bedsit, the independent room in which I had space to draw and design. The least expensive area of London was Muswell Hill in the north of the city. It was not difficult to find accommodation, people needed income and were often advertising the smallest room in the house, to let. The owner was very pleasant and the house quiet. The small room was looking down on a simple garden and I even had a cooking ring to warm up some food. For the first time in my life, I had my own room, a psychological revelation! I paid £3 a week and the cost of the bus to my college was six pence, each way. I enjoyed watching the world go by on my long 45 min. journey to the centre of London. The college was in Shaftesbury Avenue next door to the big bookshop Foyles where I loved spending my lunch hours. On the corner of Oxford Street was the big Lyons Corner House. I liked walking in and looking at the varied display of dishes so different from anything I knew in Poland. When I had spare cash I indulged in a piece of apple pie with custard, the dish most delicious!

At college most of the girls were English, pretty and friendly but keeping their own company. One girl was like myself from far away. She came from Jamaica and was going to study the three years course. Audrey became my close friend and we supported each other when in difficulty. Her radiant personality and positive attitude was welcomed specially through our first winter in London. Never before had I experienced so much fog, rain and specifically English dampness. The fog was sometimes so dense that the

La Donna, *painting on wood*

conductor of the bus walked in front of it to help the driver move through the traffic.

Our best but most demanding teacher of pattern making was Miss Wirska. She was of small stature, neatly dressed, and never smiled. I wondered if she was living in the shadow of some terrible experience which left her permanently sad. She was Polish and one day invited me to her home and told me the story going back to the war time. The war destroyed her life when her fiancée was murdered in the concentration camp. She did not know that he was dead and kept sending him food parcels although she never received the acknowledgement. Only, after the war she discovered the truth. From then on she devoted herself to professional work in the fashion world. She gained her experience of a particular method of pattern cutting in Paris, in the famous fashion house of Balenciaga. An excellent teacher who expected from her students the best possible results. Miss Wirska understood my approach to fashion design and saw how the past experience in art helped to approach the subject through colour, shape and texture. She liked my designs very much.

I disliked intensely all sewing and the necessary, immaculate finishing of each detail. It bored me and I was not good at it but it had to be done if I was going to get my diploma in a shorter time than the three years.

During my second year, I had to choose the subject for my thesis. My choice was thirteenth-century Russian costume. I spent many Saturdays in the Victoria and Albert Museum, in the wonderful library, placed deep within the building and far from the noise of the outside world. I loved V&A where, in each of the exhibition rooms, sat and invigilated an old Polish army man. I was always greeted with an elegant bow and smile.

The finished thesis was bound in a red colour and was approved with high marks by the examiners. The content was divided into

Singularity, *wall hanging*

two parts, the first one consisted of the study of the Russian costumes, and the second had my own designs inspired by these costumes. The idea of using the very simple long vestments of the saints came from the Russian icons of which reproductions I knew. V&A had excellent books on the subject and I was able to reproduce some of them, by hand, for my thesis. I was beginning to enjoy the subject but deep in my heart, I knew that making art and painting pictures would always be my favourite occupation to which I was hoping to return one day.

After my second year, when I received the diploma Miss Wirska was sorry to see me depart but while we were saying goodbye, she told me about her best student from the past years who was now the head of fashion in the West of England College of Art in Bristol. The woman was in touch with Miss Wirska because she needed an assistant for her department. I had nothing to lose and went for an interview to Bristol. Sitting in the waiting room with a group of English girls all hoping to get the job, I did not believe that I had any chance of getting it. I was absolutely amazed when the letter of acceptance arrived. I was extremely surprised and also worried that my return to Poland would be delayed further. Before I was going to start this teaching job, I had over two months during which I would need to support myself and make ends meet. I did not know yet that these two months will be the most unexpected in terms of life experience. This was learning by living! My first job was in an elegant small fashion establishment in Gloucester Rd. I had to move from Muswell Hill to the expensive area of the Earls Court which happen to be full of Polish population. The conductor of every train stopping at the Earls Court inevitably shouted: "Polish Corridor". I found an airy but a very cold room in an elegant house run by a Polish lady, a walking distance from my new place of work.

The fashion house was owned and run by a young man from South Africa. His constant companion was a very noisy Siamese cat attached to a long gold chain. Two girls and I were working in the

studio cutting fabric, making up clothes and often making alterations of some of the most exquisite garments brought by very rich
women. The proprietor did not trust us with cutting very expensive
fabrics which were ordered from some exotic country for a particular exclusive dress. One day he made a terrible mistake cutting a
velvet fabric the wrong way. This velvet fabric was imported from
Ireland and was to be made into most bizarre design of a wedding
coat! He was devastated and his fury was directed towards us
although, we had nothing to do with his mistake. I was very upset
by his idiotic behaviour towards us but decided to stay a bit longer,
to gain more experience. It was a stressful work because he had two
personalities – one, when he dealt with the rich clients, and was
"honey sweet" and the other, the nasty, suspicious one, when he
talked with us. My health was affected and once more, my dear
friends advised me to change the job.

I had to move away from the expensive Earls Court and went
further south. I found lodgings with a charming Polish lady in
Tooting Bec., Lucien Rd. The terraced houses were almost all the
same, built in the thirties of red brick. Behind each house was a
delightful garden usually with one big fruit tree which like a big
umbrella was creating a welcoming shaded space. In the spring the
blossom overwhelmed with the "bridal" colour. My room was small
but very pleasant and for once it was warm. The interior of the house
reminded me of the Polish homes of my parent's friends. They
always had lots of pictures and objects of interest not to mention
the many books. The inevitable ficus plant stood in the corner of
the sitting room and the old carpets covered every part of the floor
throughout the house. There lingered a specific smell which I
always connected with elderly occupants of a home. I was happy in
that house because the husband and wife were the kindest of people.
I remembered a room of one of my aunts in Warsaw where a
rocking chair (the only piece of furniture to sit on) was placed next
to the shelves full of old books. The corner of that room was
completely filled with an enormous Agave cactus.

The life of the inhabitants in Lucien Rd. had a definite pattern. Each Monday morning most doorsteps of each house were being washed. Women wore aprons and covered their hair with scarves. Always! This was a cleaning day and in the back gardens lines of washing appeared.

Having left my job in the fashion house, I had to find a new source of income which would see me over the summer holidays

Triptych on paper

fast approaching. Completely out of the blue, I was contacted by Mr Zimmelman who invited me to supper at his home in the East End of the city. He was of small stature, well dressed and of a friendly disposition. I felt that I could trust him although I was not sure why he wished to meet me. During the course of a delicious supper prepared by his housekeeper, he told me that my father saved his export company, which he had near Warsaw, from terrible losses.

A wagonload of onions ready for export was totally rotten. My father was at that time in charge of supervising the quality of food products exported abroad. He immediately warned Mr Zimmelman of the problem and the disastrous loses were avoided. He left Poland before the rounding-up of all Jews took place and after establishing himself in London, he had an import company. I am not sure how he knew about my existence, but was ready to assist me in finding a job in gratitude to my father. Thus I got a job which for a short time I had to accept. It involved threading dried bolito mushrooms on long pieces of string which looked like necklaces.

I had a delivery to Lucien Rd. of big hessian sacks full of the most pungent dried mushrooms which I kept under my bed, the only free space in my small room. While I was occupied by this most silly of jobs, I was listening to the radio. The BBC always had interesting programmes which improved my English. I repeated words in the best accent I could master while threading endless mushrooms. When all was done they were collected from me and supplied to the many delicatessens that, after the war, sprang up in every area of London. Mr Zimmelman suggested that I could ask a friend of his in the clothing business if he had a job for me. I was offered an awful job of sewing up skirts, with full lining which he was then supplying to the big stores in the West End of London.

Each skirt was examined by somebody to make sure that the lining was always bigger than the outer fabric. I knew that it was wrong and when I questioned the wholesaler I was told that this was a correct policy since women always try on the skirt smaller size than they should. In such case the lining can be split and the skirt would have to be discarded.

I hated both jobs, the mushrooms were so aromatic that all my clothes smelled to such an extent that when I sat on the bus or the train, people were moving away from me.

The sewing job was terribly depressing and the long hours with the sewing machine put me off making clothes for many years. I loved designing because it related to sculpting and was very creative. I thanked both men for the opportunity to make hard earned money and found a new work. This time it was waitressing, which I had never done before. The pub in Fleet Street was looking for a waitress at lunchtime when a lot of journalists came to eat. This area of London is famous for publishing all the daily papers.

A certain skill is needed in serving dishes at the table of a customer. You have to hold the big dish with, let's say spaghetti, in one hand and in the other you have the big fork and a spoon which need coordination if the transference of the never-ending spaghetti is to land on the plate in front of the customer. I had to learn the way of the proper serving, before I got the job. When I was allowed to serve, I noticed that the customers were terrified of getting the spaghetti on their clothes and used to cover themselves with the big white linen table napkins. I was getting better, but the day came when I gave the wrong bill to a customer and had to pay the difference from my own very small, earnings. This was hurtful and made me ashamed that I made a mistake. The stress of fast serving and the concentration required were too much for me and I needed to find a different job.

Apart from everything else it was a lovely summer and I missed

Those Around Us, *painting, acrylic, 2000*

the sea which I loved so much. Luckily, a new job came along – a position of chambermaid in Bournemouth on the south coast. This was a bed and breakfast boarding house with ten bedrooms for the guests and a dormitory for four chambermaids. The four girls were employed to clean the rooms, make the beds and be nice to the visitors. I had a lunchbreak to wander on the beach and dream about the Baltic Coast. It was very agreeable to be away from London when the weather was sunny and warm. The girls working with me went out to have fun every evening and, returning home very late, loved to wake me up and relate their evening adventures. The broken nights made me permanently tired. They also made sure to be in the bedrooms of the departed guests before me to take any gratuity which the visitors left. They were not interested in books which were also left by the guests. I ended up with many books, some interesting. The boring ones I used to leave on public transport for whoever wished to have them. Although the work in the B&B was acceptable for a while, when a friend told me about a home for orphaned children in South Devon which needed somebody to look after children, I couldn't wait to get there. I always loved children, their readiness to try new things and their endless curiosity, energy and creativity. Naughtiness happens when children are bored and have nothing interesting to occupy their minds and hands.

I was very interested to learn more about this home which was a walking distance from the Buckfast Abbey. It was ran by a Polish lady and her assistant. During summer time more children arrived when their parents needed a break. The owner of the home was Mrs Malkowska who before the war was very famous and respected head of the Polish girl guides. When I told my mother that I met her, she was astonished and immediately wrote to her how much she loved being in the girl guides while at school. To me, she wrote about one misadventure in which she was the central figure. One day Mrs Malkowska was on an inspection tour of the guides' summer camp. Everything was perfectly prepared for the important visit and my

*Olga Malkowska, the head
of Polish Guides*

mother was on the kitchen duty when the chief arrived. She asked my mother a simple question, *"how long does it take to boil an egg soft?"* My mother had no idea, but reasoned that the longer you cook something, the softer it would become.

This was her answer which of course was greeted with much laughter. All her guide friends felt that she had disgraced the group and later on they dunked her in the nearby lake as punishment.

Every evening when the children were asleep I listened to the stories of the very eventful life both ladies had in Poland before the war. One story particularly disturbed me. Mrs Malkowska had contacts in England through the international scouting and came to England just before the war started. Her husband died during the war and she was left with a very young son to look after. The Polish authority in exile had a serious project for her. They needed a trustworthy person and she certainly was such a person. It involved moving into a house of a Polish man who died and left a large number of precious, historical objects which he collected throughout his life. He wanted all of them to go to a Polish National Collection. Unfortunately, he died before cataloguing all his treasures. Mrs Malkowska undertook the job of cataloguing everything. She moved into his house with her little son and spent many months doing the job. All went well until strange things started to occur in the house. She noticed books falling off the shelves, a precious plate fell and smashed and when the telephone wires were cut off inside the home, she became seriously worried. One night, while she was in bed reading, the door to her bedroom opened and she saw an indentation on the side of her bed as if somebody invisible sat there. This was the final moment when this brave and without superstitions person for the first time in her life got frightened. She contacted the wife of the editor of the *Times*, a friend of hers and told her about her serious concerns. Her friend suggested inviting to the house a medium in order to find out what the problem was. The invited lady arrived and as soon as she walked in the house, she announced that a man is standing on the staircase. He wished to apologise to Mrs Malkowska for all the disturbance which he caused. The reason was that he had learned about the scheme which was going to stop all his collection from going to Poland. He wanted her assurance that she will act and prevent it. Now that she was made aware of it, he assured her that he would no longer need to bother her. She kept her word and with the help of her influential friends succeeded in the task entrusted to her. The story was for me extremely unnerving and for a while I became terrified of nightly noises. While the evenings were devoted to storytelling, the days were full of joyous work with many children in our care. On Sundays, we walked to the abbey for Mass. The friars were very welcoming and happy to show us their orchards, vegetable garden and the beehives. The Buckfast honey which they produced as well as the wine was well known for its rich flavour. Their community was hardworking and completely self-sufficient. From all the jobs which I had during these two months of summer, this one was for me the most wonderful. I was sorry to leave the two wise old ladies and the brood of lively children but I needed to prepare myself for the new position of the assistant at the West of England College of Art. Yet another move into the unknown!

My new home was an attic room in a big house in the Clifton area of Bristol. The house was on the hill overlooking the town. The room had a little kitchen which was lovely – no longer a bedsit with a cooking ring in the corner! It had a gas heater which unfortunately was situated next to my bed and when I started waking up with headaches a leaking pipe was discovered. I was lucky to be used to sleeping, since my early childhood with an open window and I had no doubt that it prevented me from more serious illness or gas poisoning.

I had a fifteen minutes' walk to the college, passing quiet, sleepy streets with red brick, old houses in which many old people lived and were looked after by carers. It was a depressing sight, because every day they sat in the same armchairs, in a circle almost suspended in endless time of nothingness. I was wondering if my very old age would be like that but hoped to die before the time of immobility and total vegetative state became my life.

The head of my department Miriam Blake, was a very neatly dressed woman who, like Miss Wirska, my teacher, also lived in the shadow of the tragic past. As an only child of prosperous parents in Warsaw she had a secure future, till the war came. Her parents ended up in the concentration camp while she was lucky to be put on the transport of Jewish children which ended up in the Middle East. She never saw her parents again. Her early life was in an orphanage and later on a kibbutz. When the Jewish state was established, she went to the higher education. She was a diligent student and learned languages. At the age of eighteen she started dreaming persistently about England and one day she packed her belongings into a large suitcase and went to London. Trafalgar Square was the place she heard about and once there, she sat on her suitcase and looked around, wondering what to do next. A young curate passing by inquired if she needed help. She told him her story and after that, it became almost a fairy tale because not only did he help her to find somewhere to stay but made sure that she followed her ambition to become a fashion designer. She enrolled in St Martin's School of Art, met Miss Wirska, became her best student, finished her studies with distinction and ended up in Bristol having married her knight in shining armour – the curate.

We became friends. At the college we had a very busy time not

Romeo and Juliet, *triptych*

only teaching but also preparing fashion shows. At long last I had some free time at weekends to draw and paint. I took part in the Annual Summer Exhibition of the West of England Art Society. This was my first participation in a public show and it felt very strange. Preparing new syllabus for the students was also time consuming but a good experience. I was still learning living independently in a new city, meeting new people.

Creativity is inborn and can be stimulated by new ideas, but geniuses are born and there are not many around. Miriam was such a genius and we worked well together, coming up with new ideas to inspire our students who were diligent but often short of ideas so it was a challenge for me. Together with Miriam, we were never without new ideas, we worked well together.

What about men in my life? At the age of twenty-one I should have met interesting men, but I did not. During my secondary studies, most of my friends had so called boyfriends and I was fond of Franek, a shortish guy who loved playing football. It was one of those innocent relationship which ended with leaving college. My mother was adamant that the subject of sex was never talked about and she censored all books which I was reading, crossing out with dark pen all passages which contained the description of sexual nature. Emil Zola's books were put high up on the shelves in my father's study out of reach. Of course such a challenge had to be dealt with and I managed to read all of them in great secret.

During my studies in London, I was stalked for a while by a huge black man, who like a ghost, used to follow me from the college to my home. It was a frightening experience which required from me courage to deal with. I made a decision to talk to him and one night I prepared my speech turned around and faced him. He was visibly taken aback but listened to my, at that stage very basic, English. In the end he must have understood, because I never saw him again.

Mr and Mrs Moss were very kind and invited me to various dinners to which they also invited eligible men. One evening, I met a handsome man from an old aristocratic family, (he was the only descendant of Sir Walter Raleigh). He was quite obviously, looking for a new companion but I was busy studying till late at night and had no time for romances. He took me on a few sightseeing tours in his custom-made car, which drew attention of every male passer-by. I was told that this, to me ordinary-looking car was custom built in Sweden. I should have been very impressed, but cars were not something we as a family had except for a short time, when after the war my father acquired an old banger which had a floor full of rusty holes. We had it for a short time until the floor collapsed.

At the end of summer, I had an invitation to tea from the Niedenthals, and there I met my future husband George Bialokoz. From the very first meeting, and for the first time in my life, I was interested in this man. It must have been the same heart fluttering which my mother felt when my father walked for the first time into her office in the thirties, having heard about her while in Chicago.

There is something magical about the unexpected flow of mysterious energy when one shakes the hand of a man.

4. Oxford

There is no better state than this – a man and woman
sharing the pursuits together keeping house

Homer

George Bialokoz was a university don at Oxford lecturing in the subject of Mechanical Engineering. He was born in Carskie Siolo in Russia, studied in Lwow and Warsaw. When the war broke out in September 1937, he left Poland with the Polish Forces. In January 1940 he was in Paris, allocated to testing aero-engines and compressors for the French Air Forces. When the Germans were about to enter Paris, he got orders to gather all drawings and documentation and evacuate to Hautes Pyrenees near Lourde, where a rosary factory was requisitioned and turned into an aircraft factory. A day before the Franco-German armistice was signed, George rejoined the Allied Forces which were leaving France for Britain. He was next working in the Aircraft Engine Factory near Coventry when the blitz night took place on 14 November. In September 1944 he joined the R.A.F.-Polish Air Force and was allocated for test-flying duties after which, the next year he was promoted to the rank of Flying Officer. After the war in 1947 he worked in the University of London investigating heat-transfer phenomena in supersonic air flow. He came to Oxford in 1956 a year before I arrived in England. He was appointed to a college lectureship and became a member of Magdalen College. When George invited me to Oxford, I was already working in Bristol and so I knew what an average English city was like, but nothing prepared me for the delight I experienced when visiting Oxford for the first time. I was picked up from the station and driven in the old Ford car towards

Oxford triptych, linocut

the centre of Oxford. At the end of Beaumont Street and the beginning of St Giles stands the tall monument, the Martyrs' Memorial. Up the steps leading to the memorial, a big truck was perched and seem to be suspended there. That sight made me laugh but George was visibly annoyed. In due course, I learned that we did not react to many events in the same way, after all he belonged to my parents' generation and was almost the same age as my mother. He loved Oxford and wished to show me the many mediae-val colleges which make up the university. We went to Magdalen College, of which he was a member, and wandered amongst the old buildings where the spirit of the past centuries lingers. The great tower was founded in the fifteenth century and the Grammar Hall is even older. I painted that part of the college much later. The painting was bought by a fellow of Magdalen College and fifty years later I discovered that it was put for auction at a well-known auctioneers. I bought it because it had a special meaning and brought back the old memories. I never knew but wondered, who the owners of it were and in how many houses it had graced the walls.

The history of Oxford goes back to the year 900 when it became a frontier town created by the Anglo-Saxon kings. Surrounded by rivers and marshes it was a perfect bastion against the Danes. One can still see the embattled walls in some areas of the old town. The patron saint was Frideswide who, as the legend tells, refused to marry the king, and took refuge in the Godstow Nunnery where she ended her life in around AD 735.

Her shrine and the commemorative stained glass window are in the cathedral in Christ Church. From mediaeval times, Oxford grew into a seat of the university with many colleges which maintain their own history and traditions. From the theological teachings, humanities and arts to the gradual growth of sciences, Oxford continues to develop and grow. Between 1959 and 1962 George took part in planning the new Engineering Laboratory buildings and became a founder member of the newly created St Cross College for postgraduate students. I had the joy of witnessing the development of that college from a hut in Holywell to its final home in Pusey House in St Giles. Around the city of colleges, grew the industries, car factories, the famous Oxford Marmalade, the beer breweries, wool makers and the paper mill near the famous Trout Inn in Wolvercote. It was there, by the ruins of the old nunnery, that I accepted George's proposal of marriage.

I had no problem with the big difference in our age-25 years! He was a cultured man who spoke many languages and was interested in literature, the ancient cultures and art.

Every holiday he spend in Italy visiting the ancient sights and museums. He took hundreds of photographs of the old temples and interesting artefacts. In the autumn, he showed the collection of slides at the postgraduate centre – Halifax House. This was a very active social centre were exhibitions

Etching of Oxford, view from Prof. Palmer's kitchen

were held and talks were given on a wide range of subjects, by the members of the university. They were always interesting and illustrated with slides made a memorable evenings. In 1972 I had my second exhibition in Halifax House. It was well received and attended. The drawings and paintings were mostly representing Oxford and were liked by visitors to the centre. The reading room had many periodicals which often were not available in the local stores. At weekends, well-presented food was available and the centre was full of dons and their wives. It was the only facility within the university where wives were allowed to accompany their husbands. In colleges only once a term Ladies Dinner permitted the presence of wives. Some dons came up with a splendid solution and brought their friend's wife to dinner.

Long discussions took place between George and myself regarding our future life together. George wished to have many children and expected his wife to be presentable, able to prepare good food and able to converse intelligently. I was to become a busy wife with many duties. University dons life was extremely active and consisted of lecturing, tutoring, supervising research projects as well as college duties. This was more than the normal job from 9 am to 5 pm! My father was a university man and a dedicated scientist who spent a lot of time writing his scientific papers while my mother was running the household and teaching, so I knew how busy family life can be. Of course I missed terribly the chance of discussing with my mother the issues of married life. Until now I was a recipient of the caring family life to which I could return if so wished. This part of my life was so different from learning what independence was all about with constant responsibilities since I arrived in England. I had an interesting – my first full time – meaningful job in Bristol and if I married George I would have to adapt totally to drastically different life. When one falls in love the emotions take over from logic and I am sure that one does not quite understand what the demands of married life entail. My mother wrote to me almost every week and her letters were important to

me. I had so many ques-
tions about married life,
especially the beginning
of it. She was so far away,
unable to talk since the
telephone connections
were always unreliable.
All the letters from
Poland were censored
and took a long time to
reach me. I knew that if
my parents met George
they wouldn't have wor-
ried particularly about
the age difference bet-
ween us. My father was
concerned about my giv-

I said YES at Godstow Lock

ing up the teaching job so soon after I started it.

My life in Bristol has been very short and giving notice to my
college was not going to be easy. My concern about hurting Miriam,
my friend and colleague was well founded. We got on well and
shared the same vision about developing our department and we had
excellent results training students in the spirit of Miss Wirska's
methods. I dreaded the moment when I would have to break the
news to her about my engagement but she took it well and, like a
good friend, wished me good luck.

Soon after I left Bristol, I was told by her husband that she had a
major mental breakdown from which she never recovered in spite
of having a drastic brain operation consisting of inserting a gold
plate somewhere in her brain. This was a great sadness to me and
one question stayed in my mind: did the horrific events of her early
life during the war when she lost her entire family in the concentration camps catch up with her all those years later and my departure triggered it off? I will never know.

My wedding. The best men: Jan Niedenthal and Mr Lukaszewich

Our wedding date was set for a cold day in March 1962. The wedding ceremony was to take place in St Aloysius Church and a modest reception consisting of champagne, canapés and a wedding cake was going to take place in the rooms of the Old Chaplaincy, a mediaeval Catholic centre.

Mr Zymmelman sent us a huge ham imported from Poland and with a group of friends we made hundreds of delicious canapés for the reception. All our guests stood around with a plate in one hand and a glass of champagne in the other and moved around the room talking to each other. It was a typical English party enjoyed by everybody. Even the traditional "broken knife" for good luck took place. I designed and made my wedding dress which, in due course, was re-made for different occasions. On the morning of our wedding, George and I went to St Aloysius to Holy Communion. The church was empty except for a solitary figure of a woman. She was about my age and quite pretty and, when George greeted her, I was intrigued. He later told me that her name was Anne and that she was his previous girlfriend who loved him for many years hoping that they would marry one day. George's mother however wished him to marry a Polish girl and since he adored his mother her hope was to be fulfilled. After our wedding Anne married her colleague from the Forestry Department and went with him to the research compound in the forests of Sarawak. I had a letter from her a week after George died in which she told me that during her shopping at the market she suddenly had a strong shattering feeling that something had happened to George and she fainted. This indeed happened exactly at the time when he died. Carl Jung said that a moment from the past can suddenly take possession of consciousness with powerful emotions that can momentarily induce an unexpected dramatic reaction.

The whole wedding ceremony and the reception with the distinguished colleagues of Georges went well. I was saddened by the absence of my parents who were not allowed to leave Poland, even for their daughter's wedding. My only sister, Ika also did not come. My parents held their own celebration of the wedding by inviting their close friends, raising the toast, looking at photographs and simply sharing it with me, in spirit. My father's place as the best man was taken by Mr Lukaszewicz who with his wife supported me emotionally from the time when, on the *Batory*, I tried to eat the banana in its skin.

We went to Italy for our honeymoon, George's favourite holiday destination. He wanted to show me Capri, the island which I knew from reading one of my favourite books: *The Story of San Michele* by Axel Munthe published in 1929. The author was a Swedish doctor who in 1884 worked in Naples during the cholera epidemic and fell in love with the island of Capri. The island was famous in Roman times and the emperors had their villas perched in its cliffs. After the fall of the empire when the palaces were destroyed, many sculptures and columns ended in the sea. Axel Munthe, with great determination devoted many years to building his dream villa on the highest point of the island in Anacapri. He rescued many sculptures from the bottom of the sea the most famous of these was an Etruscan sphinx, over three thousand years old. He placed it on the highest point of Anacapri at the end of his beautiful garden. It is looking out to sea and the legend has it that if you touch it and make a wish, it will bring you good luck.

Visiting Italy in the springtime is a magical experience because there are flowers everywhere and the wild herbs create a blissful aroma. Our small guesthouse was on a rocky, high point in the place where once stood the villa of the Emperor Tiberius. The balcony was overlooking the sea and a small table for two was covered with lace cloth. Every morning continental breakfast with aromatic coffee was served there while we delighted in the vastness of the sea and perfect weather. All around on the slopes grew majestic Agaves and willowy Cyprus trees. Milosz, a Polish poet described the exaltation of similar space in following words: *"Everything was bathed in light, gentleness and wisdom; in unreal air, distance beckoned to distance. My love enveloped the universe."*

I wished to take with me a living piece of that magical world which, I most probably would never visit again! A minute, young Agave cactus gave itself to me and I put it like a great treasure into a yogurt cup. Over the next 52 years it grew to a massive size and is a reminder of the happy honeymoon in the most enchanted place full of beauty and magic.

We returned to George's bachelor flat in Park Town. This was a the top flat to which the only access was via so called escape metal staircase attached to the side of the tall building. The flat was on the top floor, difficult to get to with shopping let alone, in the future, a baby pram. I was pregnant, and the need to find a house was a priority. George got a mortgage for a two-thousand-pound house in Summertown. Most of the houses in that area were built in the old orchards and some had gardens with the old fruit trees. We found a semidetached house which stood on the corner of Salisbury Crescent and had a big apple tree in the middle of a spacious garden. I was very excited at the prospect of tending to this garden since my knowledge of looking after nature was zero. What a challenge! The house was obviously unloved by its last occupants and needed a complete renovation of every room. The kitchen had a huge Aga cooker, for me an unknown fixture, it had to be replaced by a conventional cooker. For the next month, I was stripping the ugly,

The Oxford house

worn out wallpaper from all the walls and painting them white. The interior looked very clean and fresh – a blank canvas on which hopefully, in the future, my paintings would hang. I knew, before we married that all my creative energy will have to be redirected to the creation of a new home and there would be no time for painting. My mother's example was to be my leading light! She had the ability to make a beautiful and uniquely her own interior in our small flat in Sopot. I had a house and garden to deal with and I was overwhelmed by the work ahead. So much living space which at the beginning had no character. Making an indifferent space which always functions in many ways into something uniquely one's own is a creative pleasure. Over the years that interior undertook many changes but it was my favourite dwelling.

The garden was a completely different space for me to tackle. When I started to dig it, I was alarmed by seemingly endless number of bones which surfaced, every time the spade went in! I was told that the wife of the last owner of the house disappeared in unknown circumstances. Since I never came across skulls or other big bones I accepted the possibility that the mediaeval inhabitants of Oxford used the northern area of Oxford to bury their animals amongst planted orchards.

The garden needed a hedge to cover the ugly long fence. The hedge would give some privacy and a shelter for wildlife. I grew up without access to a garden, and had to learn from scratch. Walking round the neighbouring streets, I picked the information about the suitable and well growing shrubs in a muddy soil of the area. We decided to plant privet all along the fence separating us from the road and George, wished to plant many roses. He researched hundreds of possibilities and chose those which had the least thorns to protect the future children. We made a long trip to Hilliers in Winchester to get their advice and buy the right plants. This was my first visit to a garden centre and I never relinquished the joy of visiting these oasis of beauty. Gardening became for me an extension of my art it was also a substitute for picture making. I could play with colours, shapes and textures which complemented each other. A fig tree and two lilac bushes went along the fence separating us from the neighbours. Mr Webber who lived there with his mother and aunt had a narrow passage adjacent to the fence between our properties. In the coming years when my children were playing on the big lawn, he asked me to leave gaps in the vegetation separating our properties to enable them to watch the children. They explained that they had no need to go to a theatre as they were well entertained peering through the bushes. While the garden slowly grew and improved, our interior needed some basic furniture. From time to time an auction of the content of a big house took place in Oxford.

There was something very sad about walking into a big house where once lived people surrounded by beautiful furniture and now, it was so desolate, invaded by buyers, strangers who only cared about getting hold of one of these pieces, for as little money as possible. I found such auctions upsetting, but we needed furniture for our house and I had to stop having emotional problems and get on with purchasing what was needed.

I bought big armchairs, table, chairs and an enormous sideboard. This piece was a combination of carved elements which came from Italy and during the Victorian period were incorporated into the design which was made of solid oak. The proportions of the finished piece were pleasing. I gave this piece a lot of time to polish and to remove the old stains. The two enormous armchairs covered in an old brocade fabric became the special place for my children to play in. Children's imagination has no bounds and the armchairs were, at different times, horses or with a big sheet over them became dens or tents. Sometimes, they just sat in them looking at books. The kitchen had to be drastically changed and the Aga cooker removed. The time has come for me to learn how to cook! Another, very creative activity. My mother was right telling me that when the time comes, I will learn the art of cooking. Now was such time. I had the husband who appreciated continental cuisine and I grew up with the father who was the food technologist and for whom food was not just a sustenance but a special rich experience of flavours.

Apart from colours and textures, aromas had to be considered. Presentation of dishes was of equal importance according to my father who always, first of all, looked at it, waved his hand over the dish to get its aroma, and tasted each element separately. He never missed the opportunity to express his opinion about a meal and in a restaurant, he used to go to see the chef and thank him.

Further changes had to be made in our house because, we were tall and the size of the two rooms on the ground floor was oppressive. By removing the wall between, we would lose the wall space but gain the open plan with windows at each end, thus giving much more light. We found an old retired builder who was willing to remove the wall between the two downstairs rooms. While he was at work, I became concerned about his health. The exertion was obviously too much for him but he finished everything extremely well.

Unfortunately, we heard that a week or so later, he died peacefully.

Mother and Child, *painting*

5. Marriage 1, Babies

The world into which we are born is brutal and cruel, and at the same time of divine beauty.

C. G. Jung

It was an immensely exhilarating time of my life. Apart from expecting my first child I was organising our new home, socialising in the academic world, learning to cook and garden.

I also had to be called Margaret instead of my original, difficult to pronounce name – Malgorzata. George decided that nobody could cope with such complicated pronunciation and that was that. On an occasional Sunday, we went to Halifax House for lunch and it was an opportunity to look at my favourite French magazine *Realité* which, apart from some interesting articles, had a page of cooking recipes written by Mappie Toulouse-Lautrec the descendant of the famous French painter. Once a year an auction of all magazines took place and I was able to

On the way to the Sheldonian Theatre in Oxford

collect the years copies since nobody else was inclined to bid for them. Her recipes never failed and were full of butter and wine, making every dish very rich in flavour and calories. When we entertained guests, I always followed her recipes and everybody was delighted with these unusual, rich dishes. The recipes that my mother sent me were always simple because food products were not easy to buy and the choice was extremely limited. We were sending food parcels from time to time mostly consisting of porridge oats which were my family's usual breakfast dish. Poland was an agricultural country so there should not be such shortages of basic foods. One of the Polish poets wrote in 1974 the following satirical poem: *"Take that which you cannot get, add salt and caraway seed then mix it with that which is temporarily not available, stir it for a long time thoroughly and when you become bored stop and sprinkle this which you absolutely cannot afford. You can roast it or fry it, adding that which you cannot dream about. All of us eat it, there is enough for everybody, such is our miraculous Polish economy."* My mother sent letters to me every week and each envelope has been stamped by the censorship. She knew about it and was very careful never to criticise the Polish reality on the contrary, she always mentioned good things. Our parcels with food were opened and tampered with. When two different products were in the parcel, they would sometimes be mixed up. This was a pure spite!

Every country has its own traditional dishes and in England, the pies and the fish and chips must remain the most popular and for me very delicious. Generally speaking, at that time food dishes were simple and mashed potatoes and peas were the basic part of the main course.

Socialising in the academic world of Oxford was frequent and varied. We had parties for George's tutorial students which were well planned. He placed on a table an open atlas and told one of the invited students to signal exit at a certain time to avoid the possibility of a never-ending party. The atlas was a splendid idea of his because it gave a shy student a subject to talk about – the travels. It always worked well.

Ladies Dinner at Magdalen College was another special event. Members of the college had the right to dine most nights but wives were invited once a term at the most. My first Ladies Dinner was a memorable one. I was wearing a long dress which I designed and a pair of long gloves which completed my attire. Drinks were served in the president's rooms and at a precise time we walked across to the dining hall. The long tables at which the students sat were at the right angle to the stage on which our also long table stood. When we walked in, all students stood up in respectful silence. The president led our group to the podium and we stood by our allocated places until he read the grace in Latin. The dishes were brought by waiters and everybody chatted and introduced themselves to the person sitting next to them. Opposite sat an American lady, a wife of a visiting scholar. She also had gloves on and, like myself, proceeded to eat still wearing gloves. I suddenly noticed horror on Georges face and he whispered to me that I should take my gloves off before starting to eat! Horror of horrors! I had no idea what the etiquette in such situation was. In time, when I found myself in an embarrassing situation I was able to see the funny side of it and laugh. One such moment happened years later when we attended a garden party on a university campus in California. I was standing surrounded by a few jolly men when suddenly I became aware of my petticoat falling from my waist down to my feet. I was in the middle of conversation and while everybody was busy talking, I stepped out of the petticoat, picked it up and put it in my handbag (thank God for women's bags!). I do not know if anybody noticed, men on the whole are bad at noticing, especially anything connecting with women's outfits. Even my critical husband found this incident funny. From the very beginning of our marriage he told me to make an effort and correct my accent. His famous remark went like this: "You do not want to speak like so and so, do you?" He was referring to the Austrian wife of our friend, an archaeologist. I liked her accent very much, it was part of who she was, her personality. Her English husband accepted it while George got into the habit of correcting me all the time.

Somebody amongst our friends said that George was more English than the English! He spoke English like the English, French like the French, and his Russian and Italian were also extremely correct with perfect pronunciation. I could not compete with him and in time he stopped correcting me, when he noticed that I started to avoid talking.

I needed help in building my self-assurance and in dealing with difficult human situations and two authors were of great help. Alfred Adler, the psychologist and Dale Carnegie, the American author, dealing with human behaviour and relationships. I always thought that both these authors should have been on the curriculum of secondary schools. How can young people learn about the complex human psychology?

How will they know about social interaction and human behaviour? Both subjects, to my mind are more important that the knowledge of historical dates and the endless wars.

The prospect of bringing a child into this world was for me both terrifying and exciting.

I wished my mother was closer to help and to teach me about motherhood. How will I cope without the support of my family? George planned to have a boy first and a girl second. He was very secretive about the procedure to ensure the success in this matter. When I became pregnant, the usual morning sickness was making normal functioning difficult. The new medication thalidomide was readily prescribed by many doctors. Before I started taking it

The Family, *etching*

George read in the leading medical journal about the side effects of this drug. Asking the doctor if he was aware of the alarming findings, he was told that he knew nothing about it and said, "*I have no time to read medical journals.*" George was horrified, we changed the doctor and my morning sickness in time subsided without drugs.

Three months into my pregnancy my father arrived and I was overjoyed. He was invited to the first International Congress of Food Science and Technology. The banquet took place in September 1962 in the Guildhall of the City of London. I was invited to accompany my father on that very special occasion. As soon as I knew about it I was redesigning my wedding dress into an evening gown. The president – Lord Rank of Sutton Scotney and 24 vice-presidents of whom my father was one – wore dinner jackets. The evening attire of man and their wives, made it a very splendid occasion. I was sitting next to a lady dressed in an elegant couture outfit and when she inquired about the design of my dress which was exceptionally lovely, I told her that it was my creation. Perhaps she was hoping to hear that it was some French couturier who created my gown, because from the moment I proudly admitted my creation, the woman stopped talking to me. Was she jealous or simply bad mannered? I am glad to say that only once before, I experienced what I call snobbery and it was whilst we were on our honeymoon in Italy. We were invited to a party in Rome. When we walked in, the ladies had one look at my simple, cotton dress and their reaction was so dismissive that it made me very uncomfortable. None of these women wished to talk to me. I hated every moment of being there. George was equally shocked and the next day he took me to a fabric store where we bought a piece of silk cloth, white with a big geometrical black patterns. No more modest little cotton dresses for his wife! I made it into a striking dress and a large hat of shining black straw completed the glamorous outfit. I wore it to the next Encaenia – an annual university garden party which follows the occasion of Honoris Causa given to distinguished and famous people at the Sheldonian.

My father's visit was his first to Oxford and we made sure that he met people who might interest him as well as having time for our splendid medieval sights. He met scientists working in his field and went to visit Sir Arthur "Bomber" Harris where he tasted his culinary creations. Harris loved cooking and had a very appreciative guest in the person of my father. I doubt that George and my father would ever be more than just courteous towards each other but for me, they were the most special men and I loved them both in equal measure. His visit was short but a happy one. He delighted in seeing his daughter coping well with the many demands which the new life posed. I was happy anticipating the birth of the first child having made the home a pleasant place and the garden was looking good.

On the 15th of February 1963, I took the bus to the centre of Oxford. Melting, dirty snow was lying everywhere and while standing, at the post office talking to a friend, my waters broke. I had no control over it. My thoughts were that the baby obviously was ready to enter the world. I needed to get to the Radcliffe Infirmary, before the labour starts. The messy streets were of great help and nobody could notice a woman walking and water pouring down her legs! The first taxi I could find took me swiftly to the hospital and the driver was not concerned at all about possible dampness left by me. George was giving a lecture and was very busy (this was the time before men were present at the birth of their child). I didn't bother to contact him because the labour went smoothly and within a few hours our first child arrived. The maternity ward sent a message to George who proudly announced to his students that he just became a father.

Alex, the new baby

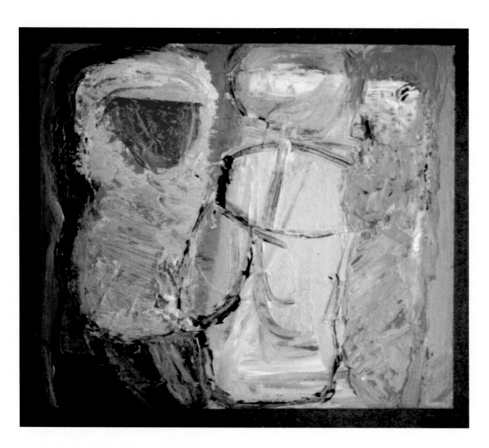

Painting on the subject of children

His name was to be Alexander George. From the very beginning, Alexander was the most delightful, cheerful and calm baby. I used to sit and watch him for hours oblivious to all the jobs, always waiting to be done. The first birth must be the most powerful experience for every woman. From the moment of giving birth one's life is changed for ever. The twenty-four hour care, and total dedication comes naturally. I missed having my family near to share the joys and concerns which every new mother has. We did not have a washing machine and disposable nappies were not produced so keeping baby clean was consuming much time. Everything was washed by hand after soaking in buckets.

The christening was planned and Jan Niedenthal was to be the godfather and Countess Elzbieta Potocka, the godmother. I had great joy to redesign, once again, my wedding dress and make a christening dress for our son. Apparently it was a very old custom and I liked to follow the old traditions. Alexander looked truly angelic in his dress.

In the summer, George planned to go to Italy because he had an idea of covering the floor of our sitting room with the marble from Carrara Mountains. Our son was six months' old and the prospect of driving for many, many hours was not something I was looking forward to. The first stop was Florence where George carried his son in Uffizi Gallery showing him the Renaissance paintings. Alexander behaved perfectly and the next day we were on the way to Marina di Massa situated near the Carrara mountains, where many different types of marble has been excavated over the millennia. We went to the showrooms and chose three different colours and loaded two big slabs of pink and green coloured marble into our old car. On the way back, we visited Lucca with its beautiful monastery and while there, Alexander became feverish and we had to call a doctor who was horrified when George told him that the baby had no inoculations of any kind, prior to the trip. At the age of six months, he got his first antibiotic and soon was well again. We pushed the baby in the collapsible pushchair all around the old city in great heat. Most of the time, he was wearing only a nappy and was happy waving his legs. The Italian women always wished to look at the baby and were horrified seeing him almost completely naked. They couldn't stop themselves from showing great disapproval: "*poverino, bambino, pancino scoperta!*" The reason for such reaction was that all Italian babies we saw, were wrapped up and wore bonnets. I cannot imagine how hot the poor things must have been!

Like most men, George liked fast driving and once in the car our long journey home had to be as short as possible. There were no seatbelts in those days. I had lots of movement and could change and feed Alexander while the car was on the move. My memory of an accident we had while I was pregnant left me worried and I did not enjoy going by car since that time.

That awful night of the accident I will never forget. We were returning from London on a wet autumn day and the A40 around High Wycombe was covered with fallen leaves. This was the road full of bends and on that night, prior to our travel, an accident caused an oil spill which subsequently was covered with falling leafs. George was driving fast and tried to overtake a slow vehicle but had to break suddenly. Our car started spinning around and met the oncoming traffic head on. We were hit many times, the passenger door swung open and I was thrown out, ending unconscious on the grass verge. I woke up in the hospital in High Wycombe and my first question to the nurse was: "*Is my baby safe?*" She was astonished because nobody informed her that I was pregnant. George was just bruised and came to see me the next day. The car was badly damaged. The driver of the car which drove into us, when asked why he did not stop, said, "*Gov. – you were not supposed to be on my side of the road!*"

The invention of safety belts was a tremendous safety asset but our journey home was still without them. I was praying for a safe return. Perhaps the heavy load of marble in the boot of the car made me think that George would not drive fast. We got home within a couple of days, exhausted but safe.

George was convinced that the best education for his child will have to be in a public school. Alexander's name was registered at Eton. George spoke to his son in French while I was meant to speak in Polish. English, he would acquire at school! So that was that!! I was horrified and could never understand why people have children and deprive them of parental contact and care letting strangers take care of them. I am convinced that if the child is to grow up a balanced, without psychological problems adult, he needs devoted care from his parents. There is absolutely no substitute for it. I was very much against it just as I hated the idea of marbled floor in our semi, 1930s house. I had to be very diplomatic, and an idea came to me one day. I asked George what would happen if Alexander fell out of his pram, or his chair and hit his head on the hard marble floor? George admitted that he had not thought about such possibility and I won!!! The case of marble floor became history! As to the public schools, I strongly believed that when we had good schools in Oxford it was unnecessary to send the child away. My only hope was that when the time came, we would not have the resources to pay the high fees.

Having a baby and a very demanding husband was a full time job and my art was put on hold for a very long time. All creativity was directed towards my child. I was reading anything which might help me to nurture his development. There were so many questions! Anything about child development was important for me to know. Benjamin Spock was the popular author on child care. He helped to revolutionise many old attitudes and views. Two of his famous messages were: "*trust yourself. You know more than you think you know.*" The other one was: "*the child supplies the power but the parents have to do steering*" We experience the world through seeing, hearing, tasting, smelling or touching. The baby's brain develops very fast and needs all kinds of stimulation. It learns to smile because the parent smiles and responds to the environment very quickly. I noticed quite early Alexander's fascination with colours and the sound of music. Mozart especially drew his attention. When

Alexander was 14 months old, on the 5th of May 1964 Barbara Alexandra was born. This was called by George: "*the Alexander class!*"

The medical profession encouraged home birth and so it was that a midwife was present at her birth. There was nothing to lessen the pain and the agony of many hours in labour took its toll. I must have pushed too much at the end and the baby was born with huge red bruising on her forehead. The doctor came to visit me after a few days and told me to have a bath. This caused an infection which over the next days intensified. I had high temperature and from the waist down I was totally numb. George was alarmed and demanded from the doctor to deal with the obvious complication. The doctor was furious with George and after a noisy confrontation, he ordered an ambulance to take me to hospital, "*to get you away from your husband's interference*". The baby and I ended up in hospital where immediate injections of high doses of antibiotics saved my life. In

Our first visit to Sopot Beach with my uncle, aunt and parents

George with his two treasures and the thornless roses

fact it was George who saved my life by not accepting the doctor's mistaken opinion. I was breastfeeding Barbara who was, like Alexander, a very calm and content baby. The amount of drugs which were pumped into me, must have passed in the milk to her and made her unhappy. From a happy baby, she became agitated and cried a lot. Throughout her early childhood she had the most awful screaming fits. Alexander used to hide his head under a cushion whenever Barbara started screaming. Very soon she learned that when she wanted a toy with which Alexander was playing, all she needed to do was to start screaming and the toy was hers! I will never know if this draconian treatment to clear the infection was the cause of Barbara's frequent unhappiness expressed by screaming throughout her childhood.

6. USA

A successful marriage requires falling in love many times, always with the same person.

Mignon McLaughlin

The colleges of Oxford are independent institutions with their own governing bodies and their own income. The college system allows contacts between members of the staff who are occupied in different intellectual fields. Members meet, eat together and share the involvement in the running of the college. The fellowship of a college is a post which also requires tutoring and "pastoral" care of undergraduates. When George was elected a founding fellow of the newly established St Cross College, he resigned his membership in Magdalen College. St Cross is a postgraduate college open to both men and women. The first graduate students of St Cross in 1966 numbered just five. I enjoyed socialising with the new fellows and their wives. During the early stage, college was situated in a long hut near St Cross church. Its next location was in the Pusey House in St Giles, the centre of Oxford. Soon after the move to its permanent quarters, I gave a demonstration of the art of batik to a gathering of wives who were very interested in that very old technique of decorating fabrics using hot wax and dyes.

Lecturers of the university, every four years, had a sabbatical leave for a year. During that period, they could devote time to writing or research or lecturing in different scientific establishments.

George's sabbatical leave took place when Alexander and Barbara were three and two years old. He was invited to various universities in the USA. From the summer to the following spring, we were on the move from one campus to another, always having problems finding accommodation. Americans did not want to rent to families knowing how destructive children can be. We first landed in New York on an incredibly hot day, it was the kind of heat which I never experienced in my life before. Barbara had to walk around sightseeing with a big nappy between her legs because she stubbornly refused to be potty trained. After a day of walking in the New York heat, she changed her mind and her mother was very, very happy! We next went to MIT in Boston and

George with the children at MIT

found a house of an academic family who were going to Europe for a few months. Unfortunately their air conditioning was out of order and it was impossible to find a company which was willing to repair it. We were sweltering in the never-ending heat. The occasional storms did nothing to the oppressing high temperatures inside and outside. At least George was lucky because the university buildings were air conditioned and he could lecture in comfort.

I had to walk with my children to get provisions and was impressed with their resilience. We got a very small inflatable, paddling pool in which they spent most of the day. Boston is a great city and its architecture is very much influenced by the European cities. The big purpose-built chapel on the campus was interdenominational which was a novelty to me.

All professors had holiday properties in the beautiful northern areas of Maine and New Hampshire. There were forests and lakes, all on a grand scale compared to England. Even the birds seem much bigger! All Americans we met, were delightful and devoid of snobbery which was very refreshing. We were invited to visit Prof. Rosenhow who had a lovely house on the shore of a lake. We

travelled by car through the hilly and forested landscape. From time
to time, there was a big sign perched by the road announcing:
BEWARE OF GRANDCHILDREN! Our two children had great
time wallowing in the lake while I had a chance to try, to no avail,
water skiing. Strong legs are needed which I did not have, but I was
not giving up and the next morning my leg muscles were in agony
from the exertion! George made a decision to travel to the next
destination of his sabbatical, Berkeley, in California by car while we
would fly over there. A few days before our departure our car was
parked, as usual, on the sloping drive of the house. While we were
sitting in the garden behind the house, Alexander climbed through
the window into the driver's seat and played with the various buttons on the dashboard. This was an automatic car. One of the
buttons was operating the brakes and when he pushed it, the car
rolled backwards into the road ending on the telephone's tall post!
It was lucky that the car coming along the road missed our car by a
few feet.

The boot of the car was dented by the impact. Alexander of
course was unaware of what could have been a terrible accident. His
father gave him dreadful spanking, and poor child was so shocked
that he was unable to cry. This was his very first serious punishment and the only one! He was put to bed and I was forbidden to go
and console him. I was shocked by the violent response of Georges
to the accident. Surely, talking to the child and explaining what has
happened would have been the right thing to do. At that moment I
hated George for his attitude and for punishing his son in such a
violent way. The car was going to be sold and a new one bought for
the long journey across the States to Berkeley. I flew with the
children to our new very tiny house in Berkeley, overlooking the
bay and the distant San Francisco. The entrance to the house was
completely covered with vines and the humming bird feeders
hanging from the branches added to the charm of the small house.
Two bedrooms were quite charming while the large sitting room
had a huge window overlooking the school's playground down

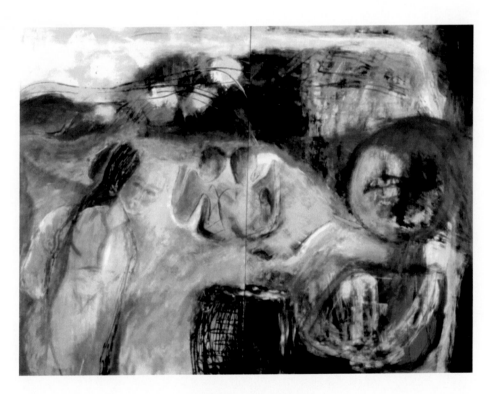

Madre Mia, *oil on board*

below the wooded area. George was a visiting lecturer at the university which had a splendid hilly location with lush nature all around. Our house was on the most inclined little street and it was not easy to walk up or drive up the slope. From time to time one heard a car making a tremendous noise driving up it in the lower gear, stopping, rolling backwards and starting again. On the whole, drivers avoided going up that incredibly steep street. On the evening when we expected George to appear from the journey which took him just three days (only a mad Englishman would try to do it in such short time!) there was a knock on the door and there stood, my husband. Unfortunately he'd had a puncture half way up this steepest of streets, just yards from home! He was lucky that it did not happen in the middle of the endless prairies.

The university had a very active Newcomers Club which had an evening of introduction for meeting all the visitors and their families. It was customary that each new visitor had to stand up and introduce themselves to the gathering. Everybody was very welcoming and friendly, our two very blond and pretty children dressed in identical red cardigans were the greatest hit of the evening. At the campus, it was the period of the students' demonstrations. Instead of going to lectures, they sat on the vast lawn and having filled the fountains with soap enjoyed the bubbly rivers flowing downwards. The children of course loved every bit of it.

George's cousin, an architect, lived with his wife in San Francisco since the end of the war. They had not seen each other since the student days in Warsaw so I expected an emotional meeting between them. Leszek and Trudie were a delightful couple with grown-up sons. They lived in a modern semi on one of the many hills of the sprawling city. It was a long trip to their house across the Bay Bridge but worth it because the vistas were spectacular. The never-ending Bay Bridge, the sight of the Golden Gate Bridge, the Alkatraz prison island and spacious, well designed roads in San Francisco itself, all contributed to a pleasurable trip. We went with them to the most beautiful of all places, the Yosemite Valley, which is part of the Sierra Nevada Mountains. The name Yosemite is the Indian term for grizzly bear. The great American naturalist John Muir said *"Its natural beauty cleanses and warms like fire, and you will want to stay there for ever"*. The clean and sharp

Leszek Piatkowski, architect and sculptor

air creates wonderful intensity of colours in foliage, sky and massive grey rocks. The valley is a narrow sheer-walled cleft in the western flank of Sierra Nevada. Near the entrance to the valley rises the 3.604 ft El Capitan, the highest mountain above the valley floor where rapid streams find their way amongst the boulders. Everywhere grow majestic sequoias and mixed forests with streams, waterfalls and spectacular rock formations. Brown, inquisitive bears and 220 species of birds inhabit Yosemite. Among these are the golden eagles, red-tailed hawks and bright blue jays. The sunrays finding the way between the high rocks suddenly highlight a tree or a rock creating a theatrical setting. The surface of the fast moving Mercer River, look like millions of glittering diamonds. We stayed in a wooden cabin for two nights, watched the changing light in the valley and listened to the sounds of nature at night. When the darkness fell we watched a spectacle of throwing the bonfire down from the top of El Capitan. It looked like a million burning stars descending to its base. We watched the small brown bears wandering between the bins in hope of finding food and we listened to the dawn chorus early in the morning. For me the experience of those two days was most powerful and spiritual and I could have stayed in the valley for ever! The beaches along the coast of San Francisco were wild and sandy and full of debris of all kind. It struck me that one could build a cabin, equip it and decorate it at the same time with the pieces of all sorts thrown out by the sea. The choice of materials, tools and objects encountered everywhere was bewildering. Millions of wading birds and sandpipers looked for food amongst the debris. If I lived there, I would collect many of these objects to make a huge 3D composition going high up to the sky and dedicate it to our modern, consumer civilisation. Everything in America is on a grand scale, big spaces call for sprawling, big houses and enormous cars. In Berkeley, the streets had pavements for walking but we hardly ever encountered walking people. The car rules the States. The three of us took long walks while George was lecturing. We did not encounter small shops only huge department stores and supermarkets. My two lively children, immediately on entering the store, run around and I had difficulty keeping an eye on them. In a store with clothes displayed on a carousel they had great fun pushing it around at great speed. I had no control over my two who otherwise, normally, were well behaved. The lesson was learned – not to visit such huge stores which look like a gigantic playground.

The Space centre in the Nevada Desert was also on George's agenda to visit. The trip took us over the mountains where long ago during the gold rush, people perished in the hard winter time. Those who survived found a very beautiful areas with lakes. The famous Lake Tahoe is surrounded by wild and lush landscape. Next – the sandy desert of Reno with undulating, windswept dunes and arrowheads scattered, the remains of the Indian presence. They had great reverence and understanding of nature while the white man subjugated it and mismanaged wide areas of the Mid-West.

Our next university was the UCL in Los Angeles. Once again, we had to find accommodation for the next few months. Nobody wanted to rent a house to families and if it wasn't for friends of my fathers – Prof. and Mrs Hodgson – we would have had to stay in some awful motel. What a terrible prospect! Evelyn Hodgson was widowed recently. She lived in Los Angeles for many years. She was our great fairy godmother who sent parcels of clothes for many

years, after the war. She called me Margy and I called her Aunt
Evelyn. Through her friends she was able to find us a small, sweet
house in Santa Monica area of LA. It was fitted with piled white
carpet, horror of horrors! The tiny garden had one tree – avocado.
This little bungalow was perfect for our needs and I resigned myself
to the constant cleaning of the lush carpet. Our Christmas time in
LA was entertaining and very colourful. The Christmas tree left
needles embedded in the pile and together with A&B we had to pick
it laboriously for hours.

Aunt Evelyn took me out to her beautiful house once a week
when George was available to babysit. She introduced me to whis-
key sour, the splendid American cocktail, her favourite after which
she served some very American food, healthy and tasty. What joy it
was to have a meal prepared for me and have it in the beautiful
surrounds of her home and the lush garden. She was very kind and
used to arrive in her huge Cadillac car, silent and spacious and take
us on a journey to interesting parts of LA. We visited the Mexican
district and the Indian Museum as well as the Cinema City. She did
not have children of her own and I admired her seemingly never-
ending patience with my two. When Christmas came every house
seem to be competing for the biggest display of lights which decorate the houses and every bush and tree. I was sad to leave LA and
the kind hospitality of the people we met there.

In January we were packing up to go to Miami University in
Coral Gables. Somehow we did not manage to pack up all our
belongings. I ran out of time cleaning the house which was to go
back on the market as soon as we left. George was at the university
till the last day so I could not count on his help. Aunt Evelyn
offered to take us to the airport which was about an hour's drive
from Santa Monica. She arrived to pick us up and was faced with a
request for organising and forwarding the packages which we did
not manage to send ahead. These were mostly George's books
which he brought from the university without any forewarning.
There simply was no time to deal with it.

I saw how worried this old and kind lady was, faced with the unexpected task. This must have been the reason why she missed the exit from the highway to the airport. That of course made her even more upset. We were looking at the clock and silently praying. When we got to the airport, all of us had to run and run and run. We were the last passengers at the boarding gate.

We were on the way to Miami! This, last part of our journey was the worst experience for me. We stayed in an ugly unkempt motel which had not a single tree or bush growing near. In the middle of the courtyard stood an empty pool. We all hated being there and made sure that we went out for the whole day. On Sunday, we went to the nearest Catholic Church, where we were the only white family. It must have been a shock to the congregation because when we entered, all singing stopped and silence descended. Everyone turned around to look at us. The place was made for our family and the children were very well behaved. While George was at the university we went to the beach, which looked lovely, with rows of palm trees all growing at different angles due to the strong winds battering the area from time to time. The sand was perfectly white and the sea brilliant blue with a haze on the horizon. Wooden high platforms were placed along the sandy beach. On each one sat a life-guard with big box of first aid kit. I went to ask one of them how safe was swimming for my children. He told me that in the water were lots of pieces of glass and he had to deal with cuts, hence the first aid box. I immediately told my children to sit and wait till I walked between two stones which I placed as markers and carefully inspected the water picking up a hand full of broken glass. The children were very impatient until I showed them what I found and they understood the danger of cutting themselves. We had fun after that, playing within the safe area but I was all the time concerned about our safety.

We visited the Parrot Jungle and the crocodile enclosure which had a big sign warning visitors *"do not throw anything, somebody has to pick it up, would you like to be that person?"* The tropical heat and the visible racial problems of the society, based on wealth and colour, were tangible in Miami. I was relieved that we did not have to stay there for long.

Our flight took us to New York where we had to change planes. Somewhere between Florida and London, one of our suitcases disappeared. It contained all children's toys and clothes.

Towards the end of our trip Alexander developed a hearing problem and

Parrot Jungle, Florida

we were advised to wait, for a mastoid operation, till we got back to Oxford. We returned home in a state of anxiety. The time when parents were allowed to stay in hospital with the child had not come as yet and Alexander, normally a very calm and happy child, was visibly frightened. The operation went well and he returned home with a huge bandage round his head which looked

Family in Oxford

like a helmet. He was going to start school very soon and when he got his uniform, Barbara had a fit of jealous screaming, the usual expression of stating her annoyance. She joined her brother the following year and both were happy at the Notre Dame Preparatory School in Oxford.

While we were in the USA distressing news reached us from Poland. My father had been expelled from the Gdansk Technical University. His personal,

Alexander's first uniform

private letters had been censored in spite of the constitutional rights which protect correspondence of a citizen. Such law in practice does not exist and obviously the communist party was looking for reason to destroy the lives of people who did not follow the party lines. People who were strong and independent thinkers with patriotic and positive minds, were always in danger of being destroyed. Years ago the Polish philosopher and friend of my father Jan Stachniuk was murdered by the criminals serving the system. The letter which my father wrote to a friend in Warsaw was, like his other letters, intercepted and read. In it was a joke which had political implications and was being used as the reason for expulsion. I wonder how it was possible that the chancellor of the university did not ask the help of a lawyer to defend their most illustrious scientist, but went along with the party's order to remove my father from his position. This will remain a very "black" moment in the history of the otherwise excellent educational establishment. Twenty years later the Minister of Education wrote a letter to my father expressing his regret at the unjust dismissal, congratulating him on his scientific achievements and the international recognition. The scientific world in the field of Food Science was appreciating my father's achievements but in his own country he was *persona non grata*. The scientist from Britain Prof. Blanchfield said the following about my father: "*To describe his achievements is to do him less than justice. He was a wonderful companion with a great sense of fun but he was also a philosopher whose concern for the welfare of his fellow beings was the mainspring of his personal life.*"

It was a very distressing time for us and we tried to support my parents in whatever way possible. George wrote a letter to *The Times* about the persecution of scientists. I could imagine the terrible loneliness of a man of great stature who suddenly is hopelessly discarded. One wonderful, caring Mrs Kwiatkowska, an employees of the University, fought to secure a pension for my father. People like her are unique. They are prepared to risk their own wellbeing and perform good deeds which help to restore our faith in humanity. My father was a strong and determined scientist and for the next 29 years till the end of his life he continued his work from his study, at home. At the end of every year, the chancellor of the university received a list of publications and reviews which my father produced. He was respected abroad and his colleagues visited him and appreciated his constant involvement in the important research dealing with the Food Technology.

However, in his own country he was considered as unsuitable to have contact with the young generation of future scientists. If he left Poland after the war, his scientific life would have been truly successful and his brilliant and creative mind appreciated.

Another tragedy followed and our family life was shattered again when suddenly, in March 1969, George died. Two of his colleagues died on the same day. All of them developed heart problem as a result of physical overwork in their gardens. The memory of the day when George became unwell will stay with me forever, because I believe that his life could have been saved if his doctor acted as he should have and sent him to hospital straight away. However, in spite of my persistent request for help, he refused to see my point which was that George was suffering of a heart problem and needed

My father in his study/ bedroom in Sopot

hospitalisation. Instead, he kept administering the painkillers and advised George to take rest. George's pain intensified during the next hours and in the middle of the night, he lost consciousness. The ambulance arrived within minutes and the men were trying to resuscitate him. Meanwhile I ran to my neighbour Dorothy Horgan who immediately came over and we sat praying and listening to the men upstairs, doing their best to resuscitate him to no avail.

When they carried him downstairs to the ambulance all I was able to say was *"please do all you can to bring him back, we have two little children"*. He was in a sitting position with his head hanging on his chest and looked as if he was asleep. I just could not accept the possibility of his death. Another neighbour arrived and both of them went upstairs to change the bed sheets while I just sat in a total stupor. They encouraged me to go to bed and try to sleep before the day dawned and the children woke up.

In the morning, the call from hospital had devastating news that he had died. I had to see him because, I could not believe the awful news. Dorothy looked after the children while I went to the mortuary. I had no family to help me at this time of terrible distress but my friends were of enormous help. I was walking as if in another reality, functioning like an automaton. I told the children that their father had gone to Heaven and to my great relief both of them accepted it well. Their school was immensely supportive. I am not sure how the doctor had the courage to come and see me after what I considered was an unforgivable neglect. If I had a gun, I would have killed him. He was sorry and handed me the death certificate, on which he stated that George died of coronary thrombosis. He could have been saved, so said many people I spoke to. I tried to sue the doctor but it would have been very costly and in the end the insurance, which the doctors have, would have saved him from any inconvenience. Apart from anything else the court would have taken into account my relatively young age and possibility of re-marrying. Such was the verdict of the best barrister in Oxford who went into my case with great care.

Portrait of Barbara

I had to go to the Registry in the centre of the city to register my husband's death. Elsie Wilson, a retired nurse and a friend, went with me. We sat in the waiting room while a young woman walked in full of joy and smiles. She was registering the birth of her first child. The happiness and the misery in one small room!! After the funeral to which I did not take the children, the three of us went through the time of great insecurity. We slept together in one bed for some time and it was very reassuring and comforting. I was having stupendous nightmares of collapsing walls of our home. I would jump out of the bed, in the middle of the nightmare and support the wall of the bedroom with both hands, till I woke up suddenly, happy that all was well in reality. George had a mortgage which he paid every month and I had absolutely no idea if we would still have a house to live in after his death when the payments have stopped. Dorothy once more showed her true Christian kindness and offered hospitality to us if we were homeless.

As it happened, George had a life insurance which paid the remaining mortgage loan. I am most probably, the last generation of wives who are kept ignorant in the financial matters.

My parents suggested that we return to Poland, and George's cousin in San Francisco invited us also to emigrate to the USA. All the suggestions I carefully considered. Above all, I had to think what was best for my two little ones. What was to be their future if we moved to another country? I always consulted close and well-wishing friends. Many of them had more experience of life than myself. Their advice would have had objectivity which I did not have. My thinking could not be logical, it was charged with desperation and sadness. Eventually I made the decision to stay in Oxford which I thought to be the best for all three of us. I got a pension from the university and in time would look for a job to supplement it. The children could go to schools in the city and would not go to a boarding school which for me has been a constant concern since their birth.

7. Marriage 2

Marriage is the triumph of imagination over intelligence.
The second Marriage is the triumph of hope over experience.

Anon.

The time came when I needed to reconnect with my art. Together with the children, we played with artistic creations and my return to art was through experimenting with paper cut-outs. These colourful decorations belong to the long tradition of the Polish Folk Art.

In some districts of Poland colourful cut-outs made by women decorated the walls of their huts. There was great symmetry in the designs but I was going to use different papers to make my own version of the cut-out. Many years later, once more I return to the cut-outs and used them as an integral part of a painting. At this early stage the idea came through making art with children. A paper collage I was told, belonged to the field of crafts.

I joined the Oxford Craft Guild in order to exhibit my cut-outs in their annual show. I used a variety of different papers, thin tissue and coarser coloured papers to achieve good contrast. The finished work was that of structured compositions. I knew that it was going to be the beginning of my return to art, time permitting! Our life, so changed, slowly settled and the precious few hours devoted to my art were restoring my mental balance after George's death.

There were many invitations to parties and gatherings and I was meeting new people. When the summer holidays arrived, we were invited by Prof. and Mrs Palmer to visit them in the glorious mountains near Salzburg. The weather was perfect, their hospitality reflected their kindness. They had a lovely garden with young fruit trees. My boisterous children pretended to be monkeys and swung from a young cherry tree, breaking some branches. Our hosts were upset but tried not to show it. I was of course very embarrassed.

Prof Palmer was *persona non grata* at the university in Oxford because he dared to point out the mistakes which the famous archaeologist Evans made with the dating of the excavations in Knossos. How dared he point out the mistakes! Evans was living comfortably in Oxford while his assistants were sweating in the heat of Crete excavations. He waited to receive the results and published them to the great acclaim. He is known in the archaeological books as the most famous person who excavated Knossos.

The autumn term started, and the children were back at school which they both liked. I was invited to a party at which was present a social worker, a friend of a friend, who suggested that I should meet a man – Neil Smith – who was looking for lodging with a family.

With Neil Smith in 1971 (above)

With my sister Ika and Peter – their wedding in 1971 (right)

In the sixties, there was a sudden exit of number of priests from the Roman Catholic Church. Neil Smith was one of them. After 20 years of priesthood during which he worked in the Keel University and later as a chaplain to a borstal, followed by becoming a parish priest and church builder in Littlemore, Father Patrick left the church. It must have been devastating for the parishioners who loved him to be told publicly during mass, "*after many years of soul searching, I have to accept that the Church no longer has any real meaning for me and I can no longer continue to live a lie ...*". It was devastating for many devoted members of the parish to hear this announcement. The church hierarchy did everything possible to persuade him to change his mind which he could not do! From then on he was Neil Smith the person without a job or roof over his head. His brother rejected him but his sister Monica stood by his decision. He made a very brave decision to stay in the area and became a barman at the local pub. He always wanted to serve the people and improve their lives and when a chance of becoming a warden in the Blackbird Leys, he accepted it readily. He was a man of ideas and a natural leader. BBC made a programme in which Malcolm Muggeridge interviewed the famous Neil Smith.

I agreed to meet him out of curiosity. He arrived in a sport MG car, wearing a black cape, looking like an actor who just stepped out of a film set. From the start I liked him. There was an honesty and straightforwardness about him but also kindness and modesty. It took me a while of soul searching before I could make a decision to accept Neil as a lodger in our home. Was it going to be right for the children? Did I want extra work which would take me away from my art? Perhaps a man around the house was a good idea. Questioning went on and on. I have no recollection of how I arrived at the decision which was going to change our lives for the next eight years. Neil moved in, the children were accepting the change and were behaving well. His work consisted of a split schedule – work till lunchtime, home for lunch and back to work for 7 pm. He returned home after 10 pm. He liked being with us and at weekends

About the Feast, *painting*

we went together for walks. Over time, the children became very fond of him and it was their suggestion that he should become their new father. All Neil's close relationships were with men and it became soon obvious that a close relationship with a woman was a novelty for him. We got married and, he became a loving partner. He was trying to be strict with the children and I was often defending their behaviour which he did not like. There were disagreements, of course as they are in every family. My children were most important to me. Some of my Catholic friends were horrified that I married a man who in their eyes was still a priest. They rejected me as their friend and I accepted their decision. When we acquired a Ford camper van we went on weekend expeditions and in the summer travelled in it to Poland, to visit my parents. My mother loved Neil from the moment she met him and with my father he shared many views and had lively discussions. Neil related well to having a family and even learned some sentences in Polish with which he

One holiday in Sopot, our family

delighted the ladies living next door to my parents. I could well understand why he was loved as Father Patrick by many women of his parish. We went to my parents every summer, my mother was looking forward to our visit. The Polish world was completely new to Neil and, when we exchanged dollars and bought him a suit for the princely sum of $5, his astonishment was complete. While we had the big camper van, we were able to carry with us all sorts of objects which my parents were not able to buy. I got a letter from my father in 1979 with the following sentence *"I was hopping with joy because I found, in a shop, white envelopes which were not available for many months, but I am*

Alexander and Barbara on Strybog with my parents

still unable to find the ribbon for my old typewriter, so please bring one when you come." Our family wrote letters all the time and my father had many contacts with scientists abroad with whom he kept in touch, especially after his expulsion from the University. Every year, before we left for Poland I made lists of objects or food products which we took with us to Poland, for my parents.

One thing which worried me much was that Neil had no wish to get involved with children's schooling and showed no interest in their progress. Alexander badly needed some disciplining and the father-son interaction. I spoke about it with various friends and one acquaintance who sent his son to a boarding school, suggested that perhaps I should consider sending Alexander there. I was very, very much against boarding schools but I decided to try it. Neil was against it especially since it was run by an order of Polish priests Alexander did not like the school and at the end of term announced that if we send him there again, he would run away! That was it, but

I tried to do my best hoping that the discipline of such a school would help Alexander to concentrate on studies. Both children ended up in our local comprehensive school where they could get away with the minimum of work. I was horrified seeing badly marked homework and

Alexander, Barbara with Paul painting with feet in our drive

very limited number of subjects taught. The one good part of the curriculum was sport and the volleyball taught by an enthusiastic teacher Mr Pope. This was enjoyed by both my children and they excelled in it soon becoming the members of a team and in time taking part in championships. As to the academic side, it was a pity that the headmaster was a week man with no ambition for his school.

Neil suddenly, one day came up with the idea that we should move to live in Blackbird Leys: "out of our privileged area of university middle class world." he announced. I refused even to talk about it, full stop! Ahead of us was a year in Nottingham where Neil was going to take a one year course in Adult Education and I was going to study for a certificate in teaching in the Further Education. The children were going to enrol at the local school and our house in Oxford would be rented to a group of American postgraduate students.

We signed an agreement, got a deposit, left our cat Snowy in their care and thought nothing more about it. At Christmas we went to Sousse in Tunisia where, at a market, a man offered Neil ten camels for me! We liked the markets where apart from colourful pottery, one could buy a camel. The children had a camel ride on the beach and I even sketched some architectural parts for future paintings. Wherever we went a mass of little children followed us. A sad outing was to Carthage and a very old overgrown cemetery where twin children had their resting place. We did not discover why there were so many graves of twins since the infanticide was a capital offence in the Roman law. Most of the houses outside Tunis and Sousse were painted blue to keep the insects away. This short interlude in a new country was very

Sousse, Tunisia

Market in Sousse

pleasing but returning during the period between Christmas and the New Year was horrendous. We were returning home to Nottingham on the New Year's Eve. The flight was unable to take off from Tunis due to fog over England and we sat at the airport for many hours. The place was completely deserted except for our group of passengers, like us, waiting to board the flight. When, eventually, we took off we were informed that the airplane would land in Gatwick, not Manchester, where our car was parked. Upon landing, we would be taken by bus to Manchester. I had most awful cold and the flight caused a great deal of ear pain. The journey in the end took a day and a night.

By the time we got back to Nottingham our memory and joy after the holiday became history! The lesson was learned – never to travel at Christmas or the New Year.

Our flat which we rented in Nottingham was situated in a leafy area, near the castle. It had an upright piano in the corner of the sitting room and Barbara announced that she would like to learn to play. She had to wait till we returned to Oxford where Eve Barsham, a friend was giving lessons.

I never thought that we might have problems upon returning home, how naïve I was! We found our house in a terrible state. The man to whom we rented our home, was not there, instead in each of the two bedrooms sat two girls and on the desks had small heaters on full blast (this was June!). As soon as we arrived, both of them, without a single word put their books into the backpacks and left the house. They refused to talk not even a goodbye, they just walked out! The sitting room ceiling had black prints of big hands. The two old Victorian armchairs had broken legs. The attic, in which we stored our belongings was forcefully entered, the padlock removed. Dirty clothing was scattered all around. The devastation of our once pleasant home was so shocking that I suffered some sort of breakdown. The doctor prescribed Valium and lots of sleep. Neil went back to work and the children back to school while I was sleeping off the shock, instead of sorting out the house. The refuse disposal van arrived and when I opened for them the garage door they were silent in astonishment. Big sacks of saw dust and empty tins from the cat food filled the garage with a terrible smell. Broken furniture was just thrown in. The big metal climbing frame in the garden had cracks in it. We were unable to find the man who rented our house and the many books which were left behind were no consolation for the damage done. The telephone bill was spectacular as was the energy bill. All their books, mostly on arts subjects were on every page underlined with ink pens of different colours.

I was always puzzled by the fact that a lot of humans do not care about things which do not belong to them. This applies to most rented houses which are usually neglected by the tenants. This was my experience at an early age when all around in Poland, people living in somebody's house showed no interest in caring for it. Right through my long life I experienced the same indifference towards property which was not owned. Our neighbour, Mr Webber, was greatly relieved to see us back home and told us many stories about the goings-on. The man who rented the house, had a heavy motorcycle which disturbed everybody's night. They made film sets in the garden, hence the sacks of sawdust. In it they buried a person and filmed with heavy cameras which were screwed with clamps to the metal climbing frame, cracking it.

As soon as my health returned, I began renovating our house. Neil's health was troubling me, his sudden bursts of bad temper

Memory of Sousse

were not normal. His approach to my children was also unusually critical and they started to avoid him or not talk when he was at home. What used to be a lively conversation at meal times was now a long silence interrupted only by the sound of eating. He was going to start a new job of the Adult Education Organiser and was expected to attend meetings and create a whole new programme of activities. This was a very busy time for both of us – I was about to start teaching Art in the School of Occupational Therapy in Headington. I was very excited about this appointment but very worried about Neil's state of mind. He agreed to seek medical advice and our wonderful doctor M. Kenworthy-Browne ordered many tests which resulted in a devastating diagnoses. Neil had chronic leukaemia and the prognosis was not good. Doctors did not wish to give any prognosis but the medical journals in my college informed me that a patient with that condition, can survive for maximum of eight years. My children took the information surprisingly well and their attitude full of empathy towards Neil astonished me. They showed a great deal of care and tried to be well behaved most of the time, avoiding irritating situations. From then on, our life was punctuated with visits to hospital for treatment, and creating and maintaining a restful home environment. Neil continued working as hard as always. He even managed to cut down smoking and eventually gave it up altogether.

At Christmas time we had always some visitors who joined us for the Polish and English celebrations. Sometimes my sister joined us with her wonderful husband Peter. He was a Norwegian architect, tall, handsome softly spoken with an agreeable and very friendly disposition. Peter was, a great joy to be with and my children played with him as if he was their age companion. When Peter and Ika invited them one winter for skiing in Norway, they both could not wait to go. Sometimes in life, the anticipation proves better than the actual happening. In this case, the fun which they had was much greater. Not only did they have a chance to ski for the first time but they made an igloo in the deep snow. Neil and I also went one summer to Oslo on the way to Poland where we joined my children already staying with my parents. It was the mid-summer and the sun in Norway did not set till very late at night, or rather early in the morning. It was one of those unexpected experiences when Nature surprises you. The birds also had a very short night! We sat, chatted, drunk lots of Aquavit and expected the night time to come. We were ready to sleep after the long voyage from Newcastle to Oslo. In the end it was our shortest night of the summer. From Oslo we travelled with Ika and Peter to my children in Sopot. As always we found everybody in great shape, only my father admitted to me that the energetic time with the children was having an effect on his heart, but he quickly added that it was so special to have the precious time with them that he was grateful and treasured it. We had to rent a room in the neighbourhood to sleep in and joined the family each morning for breakfast. The breakfast table was each morning prepared for a feast. In front of every place at the table was a big plate with mixture of different foods like ham, cheese, sliced tomatoes, etc. She wanted to make sure that we all ate well and were ready for another active day. Each day was planned by my mother and we submitted completely to her ruling. If the weather was good, we went to the beach otherwise, the woods and the lake Tuchom awaited us. The children had to pick some herbs in the woods, mostly Hypericum Perforatum which she stored in pillow cases on top of the wardrobe in the sitting room. Throughout the winter months she used the herbs to make tea. The children enjoyed their time with the grandparents and learned a lot. Their Polish was reasonably good encouraged by my parents. One summer we returned to England by boat and it brought back memories of my very first trip to Tilbury at the age

Breakfast time in Sopot

of 21. Neil's health was gradually deteriorating and he needed a blood transfusion periodically. He was prone to infections which were the side effects of the Leukaemia. He was a fighter and never gave in to feeling sorry for himself working till the last day. In April 1980 my father arrived for a short visit. As always, he kept writing, looking up information in the many books we had and supported me, at the time when Neil took to bed with one of his chest infections. When his breathing became difficult, the ambulance took him to hospital. We followed the ambulance in our car and stayed throughout the various tests which he was undergoing. My father was astonished at the great efficiency and care which was provided. Neil was deteriorating and was placed in the intensive care department. I took my father back home and we were both very concerned about Neil's poor condition. During the night, we had a phone call that he died and will be laid out for us to see him for the last time. The finality of death is always painful and for me especially so. Throughout Neil's illness the children showed great understanding and sympathy towards their stepfather. I have no doubt that he loved his life with us and that we contributed to his wellbeing throughout the eight years we were together.

The children were in their teens and both had a busy life with school, weekend jobs and volleyball, which was organised in their school by Mr Pope. For both of them it was their favourite occupation although Alexander equally loved mechanical things. Taking apart an old radio or some other object was fun for him. Barbara was learning the piano and got to grade six before giving it up. I was witnessing the growth of two very special human beings who in time chose to work in caring professions and I often wondered if it happened because they experienced, since early childhood vulnerability of human life. They developed great empathy towards people in difficulty. When Barbara was in the primary school she went to defence of the small boy who was being bullied by a group of big lads. He was visiting with his parents from the USA and was at that school for a short time. He was of small stature wearing glasses and

obviously overwhelmed by the novelty of the school. Many years later
there was a knock on our door and
the young man introduced himself
to me. He was the same, little boy,
now almost grown up wishing to see
Barbara to thank her for defending
him from the group of aggressive
boys. He never forgot her support at
that difficult time. Unfortunately,
she was by then studying at
Southampton University and they
never met. After Neil's death, I got
a small pension which needed to be

*Volleyball tournament, playing
for Cherwell School, MVP awards*

supplemented with extra teaching in community centres. Each area of
Oxford had such centre and I was able to offer different kind of art
sessions. My favourite one was "Making Art for Grandparents and
their Grandchildren". I was not sure if we would get enough people
to attend such sessions, but I was surprised by the number of
interested participants. It was a delightful experience. Children have
no self-consciousness about being creative, always ready to draw and
paint. At my sessions, they were encouraging their grandparents who
would have been otherwise very restrained and cautious. Picasso said

that it takes the
whole lifetime to
return to painting
like a child again.
It is often the case
that the last crea-
tions of an artist
are the most
enchanting in
their simplicity
and expression.

*Bianca, Freddie and
Christopher, my grand-
children, doing art*

8. France

*Everything that irritates us about others can lead us to an
understanding of ourselves.*

Carl Jung

André and Ilse Pertoka became my friends quite accidentally.
George's cousin was married to Trudi who lived in Zurich before
the war. While at school, she met Ilse and they became the lifetime
friends. Trudi became an art historian specialising in the Indian
Art, while Ilse became an artist – a graphic designer and a sculpt-
ress. Although separated by thousands of miles, they found each
other again after the war. Ilse worked in Paris, employed in the
design establishment and in her spare time continued making
sculptures. When she met André they decided to get married in
spite of many years difference between them.

He was much younger, but they shared great interest in Indian
religions and went together on pilgrimage to India. André was a
poet and a writer with
unorthodox ideas about
many things. Ilse went
along with his plans
which meant that their
life will be organised
according to his wishes.
He was a quick-tempered
man. Ilse accepted that
she will not have a home
in the traditional sense
of the word. They lived

André and Ilse Pertoka

in vehicles of many kind, changing them according to the new requirements. Not having a permanent abode meant that he could move to a new destination, visit a particular museum or a library. He was studying and writing about the meaning of a particular colour or a symbol. They travelled all over Europe and stopped where they wished. When they visited us in Oxford, their home was a Second World War radio station – a sort of heavy Land Rover with the trailer covered with a tarpaulin. Ilse was small enough to fit under the tarpaulin if she wanted to create her clay sculptures. The vehicle had seats which converted into beds at night and somewhere there was a typewriter and a printer which André used for putting together his poems and essays. After this heavy vehicle, came a barge. André knew exactly what was needed for their free life without constrains of a permanent home requiring expenditure and care. The barge allowed them to have much more space and they could ventured down the European water ways. Ilse wanted to help me with an exhibition for which she found a venue in Paris. An International Language Centre had a good exhibition space and in 1977 I was hanging my pictures there. I have no recollection of transporting them to Paris! The memory plays tricks. While it was taking place, I stayed with Ilse and André on their barge which was moored in the centre of Paris. The memories of sleeping on the boat's hard floor while sailing with father, came back to me. The only alarming part of sleeping on that barge was the loo facilities which consisted of a urinal behind a flimsy curtain!

Every morning, André got on his folding bicycle and went to buy the obligatory baguette for breakfast. A strong aromatic coffee was served in the customary, fine bowls.

After a few years, André came to conclusion, that a four wheel vehicle was, after all, a more practical way of getting to their destinations. He always came to England to acquire the next "home on wheels" and the next one was the old bus which long ago, probably in the fifties was used to transport children to school. It had to be specially adapted because over the years, they collected many books for which shelving was needed. A new printer also needed space and Ilse would have more space for her sculpting. Whenever she finished a piece of work, they looked for a potter who was willing to fire it in a kiln, and prevent from inevitable destruction if left in a fragile, clay state. This was a vastly superior "home" which allowed for faster travel. I was told by Ilse that while they had the heavy army vehicle the speed of it was miserable and often enraged a French driver who would inevitably shout rude remarks while overtaking. André knew the signs and surprised the driver who assumed that a vehicle with English registration had in it an English guy. For the following few years I had no news from my friends till a poem arrived from André:

WINTERSONG

Presently leafless,
the wintry structures
liberate space
for a moment of erasement.
No more steps in the plain
nor dissident songs;
and starry dreams
open their eyes
inside of things.

Together with this poem Ilse has send a small drawing called "Trans-figuration".

I was most surprised when, inclu-ded were photos of a small single-storey house which they bought. It had an orchard in which their bus stood. They planned to move to it after finishing renovation. Tall

My interpretation of
André and Ilse

ladders were propped against the wall and rolls of roof felt were lying around and half hanging down from the eves. I was invited to visit them in the spring when they hoped to have finished renovation work. Until that time the bus will continue to be their home. I was concerned about the new addition to their life – two Alsatian dogs – which I assumed were the kind of security. I never liked dogs, I was afraid of them since my childhood. In spite of my concern and with great trepidation, I went to visit them. Travelling on one of these fast French trains, I arrived at the destination hoping to meet my friends at the station.

I was met by an English man who, together with his French wife, ran a farm in Pertoka's neighbourhood. I was invited to spend a night in their farmhouse sleeping on a big settee in front of an inglenook fireplace. During a charming evening, I was shocked to be told that my hosts were both in a distant hospital. She had an operation on her gut, while he had his leg, from the knee down amputated. This was the result of the diabetes for which he did not take the appropriate medications. André believed, foolishly, that he can control the condition purely by willpower, meditation and some mystic intervention. The wounds were raw but in spite of it he insisted on going home which of course the medical staff refused to listen to. I was told all this by my temporary host. I must have been rather shocked by the sad news because a sudden and persistent whistling in my ears left me almost unable to hear what was being said. I suspect that this was the beginning of my tinnitus. The next morning, I was taken to their little house which was in a complete state of disrepair but luckily without dogs! These were being looked by another distant neighbour. Ilse was getting better and would return from hospital in a couple of days' time. André was not listened to and getting into more and more awful temper, made everybody's life difficult. The message came via the neighbour: would I please get their old Citroen car out of the sloping garage and drive to a supermarket, which was on the way to the hospital? Meanwhile, I needed to deal with the little house which was cold, had no heating of any kind and no warm water. The only place for me to sleep was a big black leather settee placed in front of old inglenook fireplace.

I found some wood outside and chopped it to start the fire. Wrapped up in a big blanket which was full of dog's hair and propped up on found cushions, without undressing, I fell asleep. It was not a peaceful night, there were goings on all around me and I was so afraid that I did not dare to uncover my head and turn the light on. I would have had to walk to the switch which was a few feet away. In the morning, I discovered the source of all the noise – there were mice and perhaps rat's droppings on every possible surface in the room.

The journey to the hospital awaited me. I found a map in the car which I had to start and move up the slope and out of the garage. I was wondering what sort of idiot designed the garage in which the parked car had its front a few feet lower than its end!

I was sweating in fear of releasing the break and instead of moving the car backwards, hitting the wall in front. In such difficult situations I call on the help from my guardian angels! The car moved out, it seem to have half a tank of petrol, I had the map of the area and all I needed was courage. When I arrived on the outskirts of the town, I needed help with locating the hospital. Opening the map on the bonnet of the car drew attention of the passing driver who came to my rescue. Ilse was happy to see me and get her shopping and we went together a few floors down, to visit André. He was envious of her news about being discharged from hospital, the next day. He was in a foul mood, not surprising.

I drove home, as always keeping to the required speed only to be constantly hooted at by impatient drivers. One such guy was stopped a few miles further on by the police and I had satisfaction of giving a blast on the horn! When the police stops a speeding car, they are usually very insistent on checking the workings of lights and the validity of documents. If anything is not as it should be, the car is confiscated and the driver left in the road without his transport. After another night in the depressing, little house I went to collect Ilse from the hospital. She behaved as if nothing was wrong with her health and insisted on cooking us a meal, showed me her latest sculptures and planned an excursion for the following day. We drove to Nohant, a small hamlet with the Chateau de George Sand where Chopin lived for many years. This sleepy little hamlet was almost deserted. It seemed that all the inhabitants were either away or having a siesta. Unfortunately the visit to the Chateau was not possible and we could only glance through the railings and admire the old and mysterious garden. On the way back we visited the alpaca farm where the lovely tall animals with big eyes, were very friendly as were the owners. In France, in the countryside, people are welcoming and friendly.

The character of the countryside looks and smells just like the Polish one. I suddenly, felt very nostalgic for the country of my roots, where I spend the first 21 years of my life.

I was leaving Ilse the next day and returning home, to Oxford full of mixed feeling. The situation in which she was did not worry her because of the deep belief that life will take its course and she and André will be alright. The news of André's return to their bus reached me shortly and it was awful to hear about the necessity of amputation of the other leg. He made a decision – no operation! The gangrene has spread and he died shortly. Their unfinished, little house with ladders propped up and hanging rolls of roof felt, will never be finished. Ilse was an amazingly strong person and in her late eighties, she met a much younger Dutch man, they married, she left everything behind and, emigrated to a new life in New Zealand. From time to time I received lovely, caring letters and photos of her new sculptures. She was to me a wonderful example of the spiritual strength and determination to get on with life, always smiling, always positive, always creative be it under an awning of a trailer or on a bus, on the way to somewhere.

Lovers

9. Art: Open Studios

*Start by doing what is necessary, then do what is possible
and suddenly you are doing the impossible*

Francis of Assisi

For me painting was a great passion. Without it, my life seemed incomplete. It was a lifeline and a safety net. Terrible events were taking place in the world. The starvation of millions of women in Africa, the danger of nuclear war, death of a dear person, all connected with powerful feeling which I could express through my painting. Death of a husband requires a period of healing before it can be transcribed into a piece of art. Teaching diverts the thoughts into useful activity and the same applies to the domestic duties which keep the routine on track. My teaching in Dorset House gave

In my studio in Oxford

me a lot of satisfaction. The syllabus was
varied and included different techniques
like painting, printing, puppetry, mask
making and the colour theory. We had a
90-student intake each year divided into
small groups. In each of those, there were
a few apprehensive students doubting
their ability to enjoy the activity and to
produce required results. I considered it a
challenge in the knowledge that unless I
could awaken in them the joy of creativity, they would not feel confident to use
art in the patient's rehabilitation. The

*On the way to teach at
Dorset House*

theory of colour and its influence on our psyche and behaviour is a
huge field and very useful in promoting the wellbeing of a person.
Colour preferences often go back to the experiences in our childhood. Lively discussions with the students concluded, for example
that the colour of their school uniform became one of the most
disliked through the association. Another disliked colour was pink
because many bedrooms in their childhood were painted in that
colour. Every year all 90 students had to fill in a form about their
colour likes and dislikes. Inevitably, the colour orange was much
disliked by most students. Colours of the space in which we live or
work promotes certain feelings and behaviour. Yellows and oranges
promote active movement while certain dull greens depress most
people. The red colours in their rich combinations promote cosiness
and closeness. Alexander since early childhood liked yellow while
Barbara had no particular preference. For me as an artist colour is
vitally important. While creating a picture choosing colour is a
totally spontaneous act connected with the mystery of the unconscious. The mood of the moment and a powerful feeling guide my
colour choice. There are periods when my palette is sombre and
dark and at other times there is the burst of intense colour
saturation and vibrancy.

The students made glove puppets and a short play which we took to the centre for assessment of children with epilepsy. After the show the children were allowed to play with the puppets. Making masks which projected different states of feeling was also an important part of our syllabus. All the students ended up with a wonderful portfolios of work and the knowledge which they could with confidence use with patients and with their own children which I was sure many of them would have at some point of their life. I enjoyed working with my colleagues and all but one were a jolly lot. In every institution or establishment amongst a congenial group of people will be one who makes everybody's life difficult. In our college it was the woman who taught psychology a subject suitable for dialogue between the lecturer and the students. Unfortunately most of the time, the students were talked at. It frustrated especially the mature students who wished to contribute to the subject and express their views. From time to time, a very upset student in tears came to the art room to vent their frustration. They objected to being treated like schoolchildren. Thomasina Lawson and Cecilie Meltzer, a mature Norwegian student, were frequent visitors obviously hurt by the lecturer. Cecilie in the end left the college. Sally Croft was our librarian, always helpful and friendly. She was the friend who told me about the vacancy for art instructor at Dorset House.

Anatomy was taught by Jill Freston who was kind and accommodating allowing my children to visit her anatomy room which had every part of anatomy as the visual aid. They had great fun handling the bones and, like a jigsaw puzzle, putting them together. Roy Cole was teaching woodwork; Sara King pottery, typesetting and printing and Nova Beer, drama. We all got on well and the long lasting friendships were the foundation to the well-functioning college. I was part of that group for 25 years.

In 1981 Oxford Artists Group was formed in order that professional artists could meet and share a common bond on a wide variety of topics. The following year we organised the first Art

Dorset House School, annual photo

THE OXFORD MAIL SHOWCASE

Artist paints for a future

DON CHAPMAN

THE Oxfordshire Visual Arts Festival is now the biggest event of its kind in the country.

From May 20 to June 4 this year hundreds of artists and craftspeople throughout the county will throw open their studios and take part in its exhibitions.

In the run-up to Artweek 89 we hope to feature a number of the people involved.

The first is the North

Oxford painter Margaret Bialokoz Smith, whose major concern is the survival of mankind and the world.

She will be displaying some of her work in Selfridge's window at Westgate, painting a billboard (as she did last year) in the Cowley area, taking part in an exhibition with four other women artists and opening her studio to the public.

Open Studio in Oxford

Week in Oxford, drawing public attention to the contemporary visual arts through the Open Studios, exhibitions and art events.

Every year during Art Week my house became a gallery displaying paintings, prints and drawings. Sometimes the garden became also an exhibiting space which entertained the visitors who often came with children. I particularly enjoyed watching the academic visitors. The husbands went straight to the bookshelves while the wives looked at everything and if I had some hand-painted scarves they often bought one. I was very touched when one year an eight-year-old girl, who came with her parents, persuaded them to buy for her a print which she loved. *"I do not want a dress for my birthday but would like to have this print"* she told her mother. A visiting Japanese scholar who came with his wife requested time outside the visiting hours in order to look through different portfolios. They spend many hours discussing different work and I made a special portfolio for the lovely collection they wished to buy. They were planning to have one image on the wall for a period of time after which they were going to change it for different one. Such a good idea when one lives in a small space as most Japanese people do. A visitor from Israel wanted to buy a piece of work which required help of a professional framer. This picture painted on a very rough paper had to be re-framed and I took it to the local shop. The man I

Photographic collage

met there was the frame maker and a photographer also a member of the Oxford Artists Group. He liked my work and visited my studio during the Art Week. In time, we became friends and I became very interested in the medium of photography. There is a difference between taking a photograph of something and creating an image using a camera.

In time I have learned much about the medium of photography from Mr Provaz, who was an excellent photographer. We made a dark room out of the outside toilet and I learned how to print some very old family negatives inherited from my father's collection. The family story was appearing in front of my eyes while the film was exposed onto the photographic paper. I suddenly realised that photography was a serious art medium very much like painting. Creating a photographic picture involves composition of light, colour and objects or people. Photography became another medium in the world of my art. Oxford Printmaking Cooperative was a learning hub for those who wished to explore the field of printmaking. For many years I missed the experience of that fascinating technique. I was not interested in producing editions of the same image but the possibility of making variations of the same image was something I very much wanted to learn. My teacher was Sue Spark an absolute treasure! After grasping the basics of etching I was eager to find out what the limitations of the technique were and explore

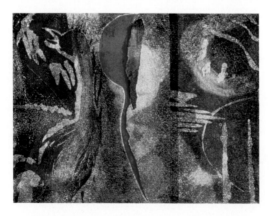

A Spiritual Journey, *mixed technique print*

it. Every time I lifted the paper off the etched and inked metal plate, I had the most exciting moment of the unexpected and something new. I do not think that it is possible to visualise completely what the print would look like.

To start with the image would be back to front, secondly the intensity of colours might be different to what you imagined it would be. For me printmaking technique will always be a discovery of seemingly endless variations. Most of my prints were unique, single copies so called Artist Proofs and if I were to produce the editions I would have been extremely bored. Artists like Picasso had editions produced by specialised workshops where they were produced in hundreds.

Paintings on silk,
Open Studio display

Sue was not only a good teacher, knowledgeable in different types of print production but she had great patience and was inspirational and accommodating, accepting the peculiarities of each of her students. Some members of the co-op were famous artists having achieved their own style and technique of printmaking.

Annual exhibitions of the members brought new students some already accomplished artists who like myself wished to experiment with printing. We had people from different countries and backgrounds. Paddy Bowler, an American, Deborah Perrow an Australian became my closest friends. Both had their distinct style and subject interests.

The young adults,
Alexander and Barbara

In the early eighties, Alexander moved out of the family home and was learning about the independence. He joined a small group of young people who, like him, were looking for their own identity away from parental influence. He enrolled into the College of Further Education to study Psychology and Industrial Therapy. Barbara, in her gap year went to Israel to work on a

Kibbutz. She was assigned to a variety of different jobs and found it all exhausting and demanding. She was one of a group of students from different European countries, all young idealists. They were kept away from the young inhabitants of the Kibbutz, supposedly for fear of contaminating the minds of the young Jews. Years later I met a young woman who was brought up on a Kibbutz and was very critical of the lack of time she had with her parents. She was adamant that her children would have a normal family life. Barbara recalled that having to look after many babies all put in one huge space, all crying for their mothers, was very stressful to deal with. There is no substitute for parental care and father and mother are equally important in the life of a child. If the grandparents are living near it is a blessing and enormously beneficial because each generation makes a different contribution to the upbringing of children. Looking at the past history through the eyes of the grandparents is more exciting than reading about it in a book. It is a "living" history. I am convinced that the time when Alexander and Barbara

Barbara (on the right) the 8th fastest woman biker in Canada

were with my parents in Poland was most important in shaping their personalities. Barbara after the gap year went to Southampton to study Physiology and Pharmacology. Both subjects were useful for her further studies of Physiotherapy at Dalhousie University in Canada while Alexander after studying at Queen Mary College became a Special Seating and Rehabilitation Engineer. Both of them kept playing volleyball and Barbara, while in Canada, started biking also. Somebody made a following assessment of Alex's play: "*He has the engine to keep on going, the*

intelligence to out-
wit and the calm
exterior with just a
hint of eccentricity
to keep you on your
guard."

Barbara was
taking part in tri-
athlon and biking
became her fav-
ourite sport. She

Alex in action

became the eighth fastest bicyclist in Canada. The great outdoors of
Canada was to become her chosen home. Her empathy with
patients, her knowledge and treatment of the whole person as
opposed to treating just symptoms, made her loved by those who
met her and needed help.

The eighties were very busy for me and I was taking part in many
exhibitions both group and individual. In 1986 I had a long break
from teaching in Dorset House and took the decision to make a
journey round the world. To finance it, I cashed my life insurance,
talked to my family and after receiving their wholehearted support
started planning the monumental, solo trip. It was going to last 99
days and the countries I wished to visit were: Pakistan, Thailand,
Indonesia, Australia, Hawaii and the west coast of the USA. The
price of the air ticket was £600 and I planned to spend £10 a day on
lodging and food. I wanted to stay in the small hotels for the local
inhabitants and avoid the expensive ones for foreign tourists. It was
a study tour and I wished to observe the life of the ordinary people.
Going on this trip was my way of dealing with the disappointment
and hurt caused by the ending of the special, close relationship with
Mr Provaz.

10. Trip around the World

It is such a delight to me to leave new scenes behind, and still go on, encountering newer scenes.

Charles Dickens

25th September 1986 – Karachi, Pakistan.

The first stop on my journey was Karachi where a friend of mine lived with her husband and two children. Josephine and Ijaz were at Oxford when they met and fell in love.

Both belonged to different cultures. Josephine was a Catholic and Ijaz a Muslim. She had a friend, a Dominican monk who after a period of instruction married them in a Catholic chapel. When they returned to Pakistan a Muslim wedding ceremony took place. They invited me to visit them in Karachi and Josephine found a gallery which was going to exhibit my collection of prints. Their daily life consisted of the mixture of customs and the children had English and Urdu lessons. Karachi is a former capital of Pakistan and its development was due to its position on the west coast of the sub-continent. The partition of India and Pakistan influenced greatly the structure of the new country. A large number of Muslim refugees left India for Pakistan. It is a city of great contrasts between the rich and poor population. When the Hindu population moved out, their beautiful old temples were soon overgrown with rich vegetation and reminded me of the old Aztec temples in Peru. Josephine was a generous hostess who took me to visit interesting places. I always like visiting cemeteries in a new country because they reflect a particular culture and tradition. The monumental tombs stood next to the pile of stones which were the poor men's resting place. The richer the deceased the bigger the tomb and all of them looked the same, only the size and shape differed. One in particular drew my attention because the upper most stones were cut at an angle which apparently signified that the deceased was a widow! The market was well worth a visit because it was not like any market I had encountered in Europe. It consisted of avenues densely overcrowded, each one selling particular objects. One was only for fabrics and clothes. The next one with pewter objects hanging from every nook and cranny, round the corner the enticing smell announced the myriad of spices. Amongst the pewter were also cases with silver jewellery and I wanted to buy for Barbara a pair of earrings. Having made my choice, Josephine was bartering with the owner in perfect Urdu while my attention was drawn to a woman who just stepped out of the doorway with a young girl. Both of them were wearing most colourful costumes which I wished to photograph. This was a big mistake! The woman started screaming on top of her voice and immediately a crowd of man surrounded us, all talking at the same time. The owner of the stall tried to calm her down to no avail, she picked up a brick and threatened to throw it at me. Josephine kept her calm and tried to explain the situation while I put the camera in my bag and in a moment of clever thinking, picked up a new film from my bag and unrolled it in front of the screaming woman pretending that I took it from the camera. The fury subsided, we paid for the earrings and promptly left the market. Josephine was told by one of the man that the woman was fearful for the safety of herself and the daughter since taking a photograph might bring a curse on both of them.

On a busy crossroad on one of the dusty pavements, sat a young woman at a small table with a typewriter. A long queue of men waited patiently to have their letters read by her and type the reply. The population of Pakistan is divided between the educated and the poor, uneducated people. It is a very beautiful race of people and their traditional garments are spectacular. At a party which Josephine organised one evening in her beautiful home, all women guests came wearing ever more colourful salwar kameez or saris in brilliant colours and sat separately from men.

Pakistan Sheraton exhibition, Karachi 1987

The preparation for the exhibition at the Sheraton Art Gallery took many hours and involved finding glass and backing for each print. After many years of experience, I had no problem putting together each picture. The opening was well attended by the many friends of my hosts. The review in the leading Karachi paper was complementary: *"Margaret: vibrant colourist"* and *"Dazzling colours by Polish artist."*

It is all a matter of contacts. An artist's work is validated by gallery owners and the critics who in the eyes of the public are the connoisseurs. Many of my prints were appreciated and we were delighted with the outcome of the show.

One warm moonlight night we went with a group of children to a beach to look at the huge tortoises coming out of the sea to lay their eggs. We went in a Land Rover driven by my host's driver. We all sat on the dunes, looked at the moonlit sea and watched the spectacle unaware of the danger which was approaching. Josephine suddenly started shouting that we must run as fast as possible back to the car because we are being surrounded by a group of men who luckily were easy to see, wearing white clothes. I just managed to gather my sandals left in the lovely, soft sand and run with everybody else while the driver was in great haste revving the engine in readiness to go. The men were running after us. I was unaware of

Images of Karachi, Pakistan:

Stall with pewter (above)

Work of art on wheels (top left)

The woman who wanted to stone me (middle)

Cemetery for the poor and the rich (left)

possible danger. What were these guys after? The driver forgot to take his gun which in such a situation is necessary. We did manage to see the tortoises albeit for a short time only.

The following day, we went to the beach along which stood "beach huts" built of concrete like miniature castles well locked up with not much inside, to prevent thieves getting inquisitive. Along the coast lay wrecks of ships wrapped up in rust. The sand of the beach was perfectly white and fine. In Europe such a beach would have been full of people, families with frolicking children. We sat on deckchairs in close proximity to the "castle" aware of being watched by squatting men intent on observing us. An old man appeared with a bucket and our curiosity was rewarded because it was full of tiny tortoises which were caught while running for the sea. I do not know what the man intended to do with them and why they were trapped in a small bucket. My hope was that they would be freed and allowed to swim away.

We visited also the new hospital which was just getting ready to receive patients. The long corridors had wide coloured stripes painted along the walls to guide patients and visitors to the correct area. It was a splendid idea in the world where many people were unable to read. The patient's rooms usually consisted of two units, one for the patient the other for a family who will cook and look after the sick family member. The window openings had shutters but no glass, to allow the air circulation in the hot climate.

I was disappointed not to have found examples of arts and crafts in Karachi. The only artistic creations were the big trucks which were like Christmas trees, covered with colour and decorated in myriad of different ways. I thought of them as the works of art on the move!

In Poland, each district had their own, distinct type of craft like pottery with traditional decorations, woven garments with stripes of specific colours, paper cut outs of brilliant colours used to decorate the walls of the huts, embroidery and lace. I hoped to find similar and unique crafts in Karachi. Apparently, the inhabitants of the North of Pakistan embroider women's dresses like the one I encountered in the market.

Leaving Pakistan, I was bothered with a question: can religion be the defining factor in the development of creativity in a society and imposing limitations to its expression?

Can religion stifle the most natural need of a human being to express itself through making images, dancing and making music? I was hoping to learn how in different cultures and religions, people express their creativity.

23rd October – Bali, Indonesia.

The next ten days were the most enchanting! Bali or Little Java is a tropical island with rice fields and temples. My B&B was in non-touristy area of Sanur and while my vocabulary consisted of basic greetings, I managed to convey my wishes by drawing.

This entertained my hosts no end. One morning I woke up with a strong desire for an onion with breakfast and, not knowing a Balinese word, I drew an onion. I was presented with one next morning, beautifully arranged on a leaf. Leaves are used normally instead of plates and children run around holding large leaves filled with rice, the staple diet in Bali.

I suspect that my guesthouse never had a European guest staying because all the children used to follow me around talking to me and smiling in spite of the fact that I did not understand them. Families live in walled areas where their houses are raised above the ground. Most are made of timber, some of light grey sandstone. All generations live in one compound and behind the living quarters is an area for burials. Everything, everywhere is decorated with rich ornamentation of surface relief. Each household has their own shrine where daily offerings are arranged. Each offering has to contain three elements: fire, incense, water. Food like rice, flowers and light were always placed on a spotless, white cloth. My room was on an upper floor and a shrine was just next to my door. I had a chance to study those beautiful arrangements which were changed every day. The aroma of the incense was everywhere. Women put their offerings on the beach next to the fishermen boats to secure their safety. Balinese people fear the sea and although I was staying in Bali for ten days I never saw a child in the sea or on the beach. I walked through the tropical forest every day listening to the birds, admiring the lush vegetation and the unspoiled and clean paths leading to villages. One day, just on an approach to a village, I met a very colourful procession and to watch it I sat amongst the locals at the roadside. These processions are very common, I was told that they represent the fight between Evil and Good. Huge masks and rich

Images of Sanur, Bali:

Houses of one family (top)

The shrine in my guesthouse court-yard (far left)

The entry to a temple (left)

costumes are worn and the women dressed in long garments dance to the music made with traditional instruments. Pleasing the demons and the gods is equally important and the offerings are made to both. The highest celestial deity is the god of the sun. While worshipping both – the gods and the demons secures immortality. It is a complex religion but it promotes great creativity through the use of drama. One day, I took a local transport which consists of a truck with a tarpaulin roof over it. Wooden steps led me inside where two rows of benches were fully occupied by women, children, hens and a goat. The chatter stopped when I clambered on and a place was made for me. I was observing the women and children while I was also scrutinised by them. I got off at a stop in the jungle and hearing the sound of bouncing ball, went to investigate. To my great astonishment, a group of men were playing volleyball. It is such a social game, requiring not much space and I never understood why it is not popular in England, the country of so many ball games.

I sat and watched the game and after a while, feeling pangs of hunger went looking for an eating place. Along the main streets, usually up a sloping verge were many inns with eating facilities under huge trees. Wooden benches and tables are shared by people who might not know each other. Almost all dishes consist of a big plate of fragrant rice with lots of spices, vegetables and unknown meat. When my plate arrived and I was about to start eating a man joined me and sat opposite. When I looked up, I had a shock – this man looked exactly like Mr Provaz. He introduced himself and said that he was German. I did not wish to start conversation and have anything to do with this man. Although I was very hungry, I left my food and walked out as fast as I could.

Balinese women have most upright posture I ever encountered and this is due to the constant carrying on their heads intricate column like offerings composed of fruits of many kind. Their beautiful bodies are dressed in festive long sarongs which in the bygone days started at the waist line and left the breasts bare. The offerings, sometimes 2 ft high are carried for long distances to many temples of the island. The most famous one, called Tanah Lot, is a sea temple and accessible only at low tide. Each temple has a guardian priest who stays there all the time. The famous Bat Temple is in a large cave but the offerings to the bats are placed on a long table placed by the entrance. It is covered with a white tablecloth and beautifully arranged individual offerings are placed there. When the bats leave the cave at dusk in search of insects, their droppings cover the offerings while many monkeys which run around are happy to help themselves to the fruits.

My room was sparse but had its own bathroom with an enormously deep bathtub. I kept it permanently filled and dived into it periodically just to cool myself. The windows and the door coming out onto the terrace were made of carved wood with enough gaps in the patterns of the carvings to let the air in. I was careful to shut all of them at night not knowing how safe it was to leave them wide open. I was right, because one night, somebody tried hard to open the shutters. I had two lovely geckos which were running up and down the walls obviously picking up insects which only they could see. It was not difficult to fall in love with Bali. The terraces on undulating hills with rice fields looking like spatial works of art and the population so gentle and full of respect for nature and their ancestors whose spirits they believed lived among them were enchanting.

One night, I went to see the traditional shadow puppet performance. As always, the story was about the struggle between the Good and the Evil. The puppets were very intricate and maximum drama was achieved with the use of lighting and beating of the drums.

On my last day I joined a group of American tourists who were staying in an exclusive hotel. The mini tours of the island were booked in a tourist place and I joined such a tour. We went to see a farm where I offered help in trashing the rice in a field. Women wearing huge straw hats stopped to watch the crazy tourist having a go in spite of the great heat and a lack of a straw hat. Lots of laughter and a thank you for me with gesture of prayer. The mini bus took us to touristy places among which was a large workshop were batiks were made in traditional way. Since this was one of my own techniques of art I was delighted to watch the way Balinese women use wooden blocks dipped in hot wax to stamp patterns on fabric before dying it in a variety of colours.

The two charming women from New York invited me to their hotel for breakfast next morning, before my departure. The luxury of their hotel amazed me and even more the long tables with every kind of fruit imaginable, and every kind of cold meat.

I was watching a very, very fat man loading his plate with sausages, fresh rolls and masses of butter! The limited time which I had for a chat with the two Americans went by very fast. I was glad to have stayed amongst the natives, the smiling boisterous children, watching their life around me. If I was at the hotel for tourists, I would have missed these special experiences of the real life amongst the Balinese. This was the kind of journey I had planned, a unique experience.

27th October – Bangkok, Thailand.

Much greater heat hit me when I landed in Bangkok where a smiling face of a young friend Rowena greeted me. She always had a kind of embarrassed look on her face as if she was not quite sure. We went to her lodgings, in a very noisy narrow and busy street of cafes spilling onto the narrow pavements. The house in which she was renting her room was the narrowest I ever been in and it was clattered with so much staff that carrying my suitcase up the narrow staircase seem almost impossible! For one night, I was in a room next to hers and the next day, I would move to some local hotel yet to be found.

As I understood she was working with a group of transvestites in the red-light district teaching English. Prostitution is the big business in Bangkok and for the Thai people it is just another occupation. Many families have to send their young daughters to work as prostitutes to pay for the education of boys in the family or simply to pay for the house purchases. The girls are allowed to leave this profession before they are too old to get married and have their own children. Rowena was very helpful in finding a room in a house which took payments each night the guests spent there. While in Rowena's street the noise started with horrendous rattles almost before dawn. It was caused by opening enormous doors made of metal panels which covered the whole façades of the houses

Images of Bangkok:

With the Buddha (top left)

Worshiping animals, elephant ritual in the streets (top right)

Entry to a temple (above)

A Bangkok Temple (left)

becoming the cafes. Next, all the tables and chairs as well as woks were pulled out in readiness for the new day of cooking. My street was reasonably quiet and the house had a courtyard with some exotic trees. The large room with an enormous bed had mirrors fixed to every wall as well as the ceiling. I was able to photograph myself through the mirrors while lying on the bed. All floors throughout the building were tiled and had a disinfected feel.

I planned my day in such a way that Rowena and I would meet in the evening and go to eat somewhere together. I had only four days and wanted to see as much as possible. The heat for me was difficult and I was glad that I did not live in such a hot climate. The first day was for walking around the flower district and the Royal Palace dripping with gold ornamentations. Once again there were shrines full of flowers and candles, sometimes at the busy crossing of roads. On one such crossing, girls in beautiful costumes and elaborate headdresses tended to small elephants who stood still in spite of the roar of never-ending traffic around them. I found, quiet streets where many pretty girls sat on the pavements putting together garlands made of magnificent orchids. I so wished to see how and where the orchids grew in the wild and with Rowena we travelled on a hot and overcrowded bus to the old district which was once upon a time the capital but now, overwhelmed with vegetation covering everything. The enormous Buddha statues lay deep in the grasses, resting happily. All dwellings were like in Bali, built on high platforms with wooden stairs leading to the entrance. There I saw at long last the trees with orchids rampant, growing like our ivy. It was such an enchanting world where children roam around and women smile and look deceptively happy.

In the evening, Rowena suggested taking me to the world for which Bangkok is famous and meet her friends. We went with two young Swedish men who were also teaching. As soon as we entered the gates of the red-light district, we were accosted by young men who offered us a variety of clubs supplying differing needs! Rowena knew her way around and we just walked into the dark clubs, stood near the entrance, looked around and walked out. In each club girls of different ages were performing on the stage wearing almost nothing and wiggling their bodies to the sound of very loud music. The audience consisted of an average looking white European man who obviously was there for one purpose only, to be titillated and to buy sex. He could take a chosen girl to a hotel with the room just like the one I was in. I now understood why there were so many mirrors. In one of the night clubs, Rowena introduced me to the most beautiful women I have ever seen with perfect, very sexy bodies. All of them were once men, who when no longer happy with their sex, travelled to Amsterdam to have it changed! The only part of their bodies which could not be changed was their voice and I was taken aback when suddenly I heard a man's voice in disguise. As I understood these girls were exploited and had little contact with each other across all the clubs. Rowena was hoping to set up a newsletter and organise them into a sort of union which would be helpful in sharing and dealing with many problems connected with their profession. I hope that she has achieved her plan.

Opposite my guesthouse was a small bank in front of which was a concrete foreground where a young girl sat with an old-fashioned sewing machine. By her side stood a young man who I discovered was her brother. He was also her eyes because she was blind. His job was to cut out the pattern of a garment which she sewed together purely by touching it and operating the pedal of the machine. The next morning, I went to buy a piece of fabric for a skirt which the girl made for me in a few hours. The next day, wearing my new skirt I took a boat – a river transport stopping at various points. I wanted to visit one of the tall temples of which there were quite a few along the riverbank. These huge structures in the shape of pyramid were covered with small pieces of old pottery or china. Inside each temple were a few Buddhist monks in the orange robes sitting on the floor meditating. The candles were lit everywhere and the spectacular Buddha, usually gold, was the central point of the interior. Silence prevailed inside were wearing shoes was forbidden. What a meditative, spiritual experience after the heat and noise of the world outside. Monks in their orange robes walk everywhere and have their dwellings usually in some green area often with water flowing through it. Such a stream has fish and tortoises swimming around and the monks tend to their environment with care and devotion. In contrast to the monks in England, where they are very busy and productive, the Buddhist monks rely completely on donations from the surrounding public. They are not allowed to deal with meat although they like eating it. Bangkok presented me with tremendous contrasts of the riches and poverty.

Huge modern shopping precincts offered copies of objects produced in Europe by the famous firms or fashion houses. They were available here for a fraction of the cost.

In contrast equally important were the temples and shrines richly ornamented and well attended. Many poor people lived on the boats along the banks of the river or outside the city in wooden hats on stilts. There was much to see and not enough time. My last meal with Rowena was in a large eating place where you walked around and watched what was cooked by different women bent over huge woks. The aroma of spices was enticing and soon we were indulging in the chosen dish. Looking down I could see various animals running around looking for offerings. Among them were rather large rats, which did not seem to bother anybody. It was not a touristy area! I enjoyed my short stay amongst the kind, smiling and laidback people I encountered in Bangkok and I was ready for my next port of call: Sydney, Australia.

1ˢᵗ November – Sydney, Australia.

I landed in Australia 216 years after Captain Cook arrived there. He thought of the continent as nobody's land and its inhabitants as savages. He knew nothing about the life of the Aboriginal people, their culture and art. The rock art and decorated bark paintings go back 40,000 years. Like the American Indians, the Aboriginal people revered nature and understood the human place in it. The colonisers showed no respect or understanding of their culture. Slowly, over years their way of life was destroyed, their land taken over and the population subjugated to the law of the white man. They no longer painted their bodies or executed drawings on the sands. When our plane landed in Sydney, and before we were allowed to exit it men in white protective clothing wearing face masks entered and proceeded spraying the interior and all of us. We were being disinfected! Our luggage underwent thorough examination to the extent that

Sydney Opera House

even the baby nappies were shaken and looked at. It took over an hour before we were free to exit. I was met by old friends Beverley and Cole Chesterman whom I first met in Oxford where Cole was a visiting haematologist and Bev., a physiotherapist. They had four children, all brilliant musicians and Cole, in his spare time built a harpsichord to accompany them. The instrument was decorated with delightful paintings of flowers created by Bev. By the time we met again in Sydney the children were almost grown up but still kept their musical interests. Staying with them allowed me to observe the family life "down under". I was taken to famous Bondi Beach and the Opera House which looked like a huge sailing ship. At that time, it had an exhibition of handmade books using handmade paper. The creative spirit has no boundaries and artists in the northern hemisphere produce similar artistic creations.

The boomerang was created by the Aboriginal people for hunting and it is usually decorated with traditional symbols. In one of the parks an old Aboriginal man showed me the technique of throwing to secure the return of the boomerang. It had to make a semicircle which was not easy but eventually I learned the way and that boomerang is still in my possession.

Forty miles from Sydney are the Blue Mountain forests the most enchanting area once much favoured by the Aboriginal people, now many elegant houses are scattered around. Walking in these forests, we came across the rocks which had incised on them symbolic

Aboriginal World, *painting on cloth, 4 x 4 ft*

The outback in Australia

patterns. I was curious about the whereabouts of the indigenous population but I had to wait for the answer until my journey to the outback. Meanwhile, I was enjoying the family life in Sydney. Each room of their house was painted in different colour. The sitting room had light blue walls while the dining room was in warm crimson. We almost never sat for conversations in the sitting room but the cosiness of the warm red in the dining room kept the conversation going for a long time. For me it was an example of how people respond to colour in their surroundings. My mother was very particular about the colour scheme in our flat where our living room was decorated in warm colours. It was only after I learned the colour theory that I understood how it affects human psyche. One of my printmaker friends, Deborah, lived in a large cabin not far from Canberra and she invited me to stay there and have a chance to see different countryside. We went to see the wild coast with huge dunes and no humanity as far as the eyes could see. We went through the eucalyptus forests and saw wallabies, heard the kookaburra birds. The countryside in Australia, as in

Talking to a wallaby

Canada, is immense and leaves one with the sense of awe. The central part of the land consists of desert where only the Aboriginal people had the knowledge of how to live and survive. From the capital, Canberra, I took the coach which took me to Adelaide. This was an extremely long journey on the roads which like the ones built by the Romans were dead straight. The passengers on my bus drew their curtains and went to sleep while I was glued to the window, making sure that I did not miss anything. The earth was light brown and huge balls of dried grasses were rolled by the wind across the countryside. Every few hours the coach stopped for a short break in what once was an old mining settlement. This was my first encounter with the Aboriginal people and I was shocked. Groups of them sat by the roadside and looked as if they were doped. Once, long ago, they were industrious people living in communities in harmony with nature. Now looking aimless, wearing shabby western clothes they were a sorry sight. What was their life about now? Later on in Adelaide walking through the centre of town I saw a group of Aboriginal women with their children sitting in the small park aimlessly as if waiting for something. In some settlements they are encouraged to create their traditional paintings and I saw some exhibitions showing these unique works of art. Half way between Sydney and Adelaide the coach entered another district still in the middle of desert where a sentry hut stood. The coach stopped and a man came out of the hut, entered the coach and asked if anybody had any food. Nobody took any notice of his question but I thought that perhaps the man was hungry sitting in the middle of nowhere in the desert. So I offered him the rest of my fruit – bananas and oranges. He thanked me, got off the coach and promptly threw them into the big bin standing by the hut. That was a mistake on my part because I still had a long distance to travel and needed my fruit. By the time we arrived in Adelaide, I was tired and hungry. My hosts were a Polish couple, charming and welcoming. I was hoping for a quiet evening and a long night's sleep after the long journey on a coach. It was not to be, because we were

Inspired by the Australian Outback, *painting on paper*

invited to dinner at a friend's house not far away. We drove and "not far" in Australia meant a two hour journey! I was so exhausted that my brain refused to take anything in and I have absolutely no recollection of that evening. The next day I wanted to rest and lying in the tall grass in their garden seem like a good idea but apparently it was not so because the possibility of meeting two most venomous snakes – the tiger snake and the black snake – was a real danger.

The lady of the house was an artist who specialised in producing wall-hangings using hot wax and dyes imported from Japan. These brilliant colours were applied with brushes to the areas which were first defined by using hot wax. When the painting was finished the colours were fixed by dry steaming. To achieve the desired result, she wrapped up the fabric in many layers of paper to prevent wet steam penetrating onto the fabric. This was very much my favourite art technique at the time and in the early eighties I exhibited the collection in three Oxford colleges – Balliol, Wadham and Green. Some very large canvases represented Oxford scenes and were bought by a visitor from South Africa and that is where a little bit of my image of Oxford hangs.

The days spent in Australia were so different from my three previous destinations and I was grateful to my friends for their time in giving me the taste of that enormous country, beautiful and unique. I understood their pride and love of Australia. My next stop of the journey was to be Hawaii and I was full of anticipation and yet sorry to leave my friends.

10th December – Honolulu, Hawaii.

Looking down from the airplane on the many islands of Hawaii, I realised that they are volcanic in their origin. They are the tips of the mountain range submerged across the Pacific Ocean. The most active volcano is Mauna Loa with its fluid lava 2,000 degrees hot when it erupts. It flows down the slopes and solidifies fast. The islands are in fact the tips of five overlapping volcanoes. My romantic idea about Hawaii was dispersed as soon as I got out of the airport. It looked like a hub of the twentieth-century consumerism! The ugly, big hotels and shopping malls were everywhere. I realised that it is a holiday resort for the Japanese and the Americans, perhaps a honeymoon place to go to, not necessary a place to find old, tradition of the original inhabitants. I was determined to find the indigenous community somewhere and perhaps some interesting, traditional arts and crafts which reflect their culture. I found an apartment on the tenth floor of one of the ugly hotels and went in search of something new! The local bus took me out of Honolulu and the crowded beaches into the inland areas of fields and tropical forests.

The tree in the tropical rain, Hawaii

What a relief and what joy!! When I saw something beautiful, I got off the bus to look around. Amongst the tropical trees nested a beautiful shrine, a temple built in the middle of a man-made lake. The water was clear and among the water-lilies, swam colourful fishes. The temple was painted in warm orange-red and so was a little bridge leading to it. The peaceful and lush oasis was submerged in the mist of tropical, gentle rain. My spirit soared and I felt cleansed and renewed. Back on a bus, on I went in search of more of the unexpected. It was not long before the sign informed me about a museum, located again amongst the lush greenery and well hidden. The artefacts on display were describing the rich past of the island. Most memorable was the costume which

Symbols of Cultures, *etching*

Monumental stone

the chief wore for special celebrations. It was entirely made with overlapping multi-coloured feathers of the birds inhabiting the island. Although this big coat was ancient, the intensity of colours was still there. The many objects of the rich past were kept by the museum for future generations. A group of women, Hawaiian by birth, were sitting round the table and working on a big piece of fabric. They were welcoming and eager to express their dismay at the changes taking place in their world. I left saddened and walked through the tropical, misty rain till I saw large fields full of – growing like cabbages – pineapples. Until that time, I was convinced that they grow on trees like coconuts. They were being cut at the base and piled into big baskets, all done by young women handling the sharp leafs without any protection on their young hands.

I wished to find an eating place with the traditional Hawaiian dishes but I had to give up the search and ended up in one of the fast-food places. I cannot recall what I ate so it must have been erased from my memory, and very rightly so! In the evening, I sat on the beach looking at the most glorious sunset I ever seen. On the horizon the huge sun was slowly sinking into the sea bathing the world in all shades of orange and red before the total darkness engulfed the world. In spite of darkness, many stalls selling souvenirs were open to the wondering tourists. I went to look, once again, for something Hawaiian, not a trinket mass-produced in China. I found necklaces made with large kukui nuts very much like our chestnuts. I did not manage to find out what kind of tree bore such uniform shaped fruits but they did grow on this island. There is never enough time for discovering the hidden secrets of the new place and on a Hawaiian island it would have taken me many weeks to achieve that. I had to leave for my last destination where once again, I will stay with people I liked very much.

15th December – San Francisco.

I have been here before when my children were small and their father was visiting Berkeley. This time, I will have more time to get to know Georges cousin and Trudie, his wife the art historian. San Francisco is built on many hills which form a splendid background to the panorama. The earthquake and the fire in 1906 destroyed the city which within three years had been rebuilt. It has great charm with traditional-style terraced houses, each one different in its design. The downtown centre has tall concrete buildings all incorporating art in form of monumental sculptures or other spatial

Golden Gate Bridge

compositions with living plants or other vegetation often incorporated into the buildings. San Francisco Bay is the largest harbour on the Pacific Coast of the USA and most of the trade leaves from there. This cosmopolitan city with all nationalities woven into its culture is a delight to walk about. I visited some contemporary galleries and was taken aback by the interest expressed by the owners when I said that I was an artist. This does not happen in London where the attitude of the gallery owners is mostly indifferent and each gallery supports its group of artists and is not interested in seeing something new. It was such a pleasure to meet with a genuine interest. At the time of my visit, San Francisco had a large number of men with AIDS who had nowhere to live. Mother Teresa of Calcutta appealed for funds to create a hospice for them in the centre of the city. The response was immediate, money raised, the house bought and the order of nuns was going to run it. As soon as the nuns moved in the first thing they did was to reorganise the interior. One day, all the carpets were flying out of the windows to the consternation of the local population. The house was to be simple without cosy paraphernalia.

During many hours with Leszek and Trudie over the meals and Californian wine we remembered the old times when our little children, Alexander and Barbara showed a great interest in the wooden sculptures which Leszek made. He was an expert woodcarver exhibiting his work frequently. When George died they offered to be my sponsors should I wish to emigrate to the USA. Although I liked many things about life and the feeling of space in the USA, I loved Europe and the closeness to my roots was most important for me. I could not imagine living even further from my family in Poland. Any choice I would make would also be for my children. Their future was my responsibility. When the time comes and they are mature enough to make decisions, they may wish to leave England to live somewhere else having been born in the free world. We talked and drunk the lovely wine, speculated about this and that, went to the enormous Chinatown for a multi-dish dinner,

Monumental sculpture to commemorate the earthquake

walked on the beaches where the flocks of sandpipers seem to play with the waves. In America these little birds are called peeps. My time of return to Oxford was nearing and in spite of such good feeling being close to family, albeit distant, I had no doubt at all that I was very lucky to live in the country which is like a big, beautiful garden and the city of eternal beauty.

I returned home on the 1st of January 1987.

Around the art world in 99 days

By DON CHAPMAN

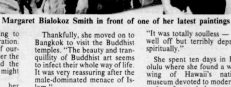

Margaret Bialokoz Smith in front of one of her latest paintings

IT TOOK Margaret Bialokoz Smith 19 days longer than Phileas Fogg. But then, the Polish-born artist had a rather more serious mission than the fictional hero of Jules Verne's famous novel, Around the World In Eighty Days.

She didn't circle the globe to settle a bet. She wanted to find out for herself what sort of role artists and craftspeople play in other countries and whether we have anything to learn from their way of life.

Having packed her son Alexander off to study in London and her daughter Barbara to take up a postgraduate sports scholarship in Canada, she set off from her home in North Oxford last October on the first leg of a 99-day journey.

"The world is a very beautiful place," she says. "But it is in danger of becoming extinct as we know it.

"We must start asking ourselves what we are going to leave for the next generation. We cannot think only of ourselves. We must rediscover the balance of life. I hoped the artists of other countries might show me how."

In Pakistan, where her friends had arranged an exhibition for her in Karachi, it was great to be an artist. The leading daily newspaper devoted the front page of its colour magazine to her work. The Government seemed keen to promote art and there were lots of rich people and institutions ready to buy.

Buddhist beauty

It was not so good to be a woman. "I couldn't move," she says. "I wasn't allowed to go about anywhere by myself. It wasn't safe, they told me, and if I was raped, I would have little chance of redress in the courts."

Thankfully, she moved on to Bangkok to visit the Buddhist temples. "The beauty and tranquillity of Buddhist art seems to infect their whole way of life. It was very reassuring after the male-dominated menace of Islam."

Federal galleries

Her next stop, Bali, made her aware of a different menace — the menace of tourism. "Yet it is still a wonderful feeling to visit the craft villages because, despite the tourists, they have managed to cling to their old ways.

"Their art is a way of life. Their craft is a way of life. They do it from morning to night and the children learn it from their parents, so there is this wonderful continuity."

She found the same respect for arts and crafts in Australia. But Canberra shocked her —

"It was totally soulless — very well off but terribly deprived spiritually."

She spent ten days in Honolulu where she found a whole wing of Hawaii's national museum devoted to modern art and crafts, and then went to San Francisco, "where I was again pleasantly surprised to find galleries run by the federal authorities like they are in Australia where you don't have to pay to exhibit."

To judge from her travels she says, there is nowhere in the world that has more to offer than Oxford. "Thanks to the efforts of the Oxford Craft Guild, the Oxford Artists Group and the Oxford Printmakers Co-operative, the level of artistic activity is richer than ever before.

"Sadly there is nowhere in the world that does less to recognise the contribution the artists and craftspeople make to the quality of life," she says.

Newspaper article about my trip

11. Exhibitions, Godfrey

All thoughts, all passions, all delights,
Whatever stirs this mortal frame,
All are but ministers of Love,
And feed his sacred flame

Coleridge

After three months of travels, returning home was a tremendous anticlimax. Three months of discovery during which I was breathless with awe and excitement. It was time to return to normality, teaching, painting and exhibiting. Before I went on my trip, my mother sent me a quote by Somerset Maugham in which he says that travels are about getting rid of prejudices which exist among nations. It is probably true but I was brought up by parents who had no prejudices and who judged people according to what they represent and what they achieve in their life. My mother thought that the circumstances often were responsible for human behaviour while my father was much stricter in his judgement and less tolerant. Having just visited six different countries I saw life there as an integral part of different cultures. People were part of their culture and equally, the culture created the people. My life was enriched by the experiences and by the visual theatre of life wherever I went. It was an important chapter

Alex with his 2CV

in my creative life. There are artists who paint when they travel but I am not able to do so. However, I took slides throughout my trip in order to have a visual record which I could share with my family and my artist friends. With the Oxford Artist Group I had a lively evening of sharing the adventure and illustrated it with many pictures which I was able to project on a large wall. At my college, later on one very wintry day, I organised a painting session after a show of slides from sunny Hawaii combined with some appropriate music after which each person was inspired to produce a visual interpretation of the experience. It was a fun session for the teaching staff.

It was not easy for me to return to normality after my trip and the silence of my home had an unsettling effect on me. It was an anticlimax requiring time for psychological adjustment. My children were now away living their own independent lives and it dawned on me that my mothering role had changed from every day involvement to something new, I was not sure what! Alexander was in London studying engineering while Barbara was in Bois Guillaume, France, studying French and playing semi-professional volleyball. At that stage, she was already living in Canada and intended to return there to study physiotherapy, having graduated from Southampton University where she studied pharmacology and physiology.

Graduation day for Barbara at Southampton University

I returned to my college to teach and to my painting which I was told became more colourful as the result of seeing such an intensely colourful world. The subject of the human situation continued to be the centre of my art. I had an opportunity to take part in five exhibitions that year. The first one was in Julius Gottlieb Exhibition Hall, Carmel

College in Wallingford. A friend of mine, Roger Perkins was showing sculptures: "A Vision of Woman" each one expressing her mystery and vulnerability. The extensive walls although not well lit, offered enough space for my large paintings which were described by R.J.P. as follows:

Sir John Rothentsin, the director of the Tate at the private view in Wadham College (his face says it all).

"Margaret Bialokoz Smith's paintings suffer greatly from poor lighting conditions. However, they do have an emotional intensity best viewed at a distance. Partly symbolic, partly expressionist, the work explores human passions. It is essentially figurative, although background and protagonists are at time confused. Figures may be outlined, silhouetted, shadowy, scratched out or painted over. Men and women seem to be in a constant state of change and insecurity in an unrestful world full of opposing forces." It is always interesting for an artist to have a feedback from the viewers. My art is such a personal vision almost always, about human relationships. Sometimes I have a need to paint a landscape or a portrait, luckily not often as I am never happy with the results.

Original design in batik

My second exhibition consisted of etchings and the venue was the Centre for the Study of Spirituality and the Arts in London. Edward

Our World, *batik painting*

Robinson, the scholar and a sculptor, invited me to participate in the exhibition in which he was showing his wooden triptychs. He was involved for many years with studies in religious experience and his reflections on the tradition of religious art were published in his book *The Language of Mystery*. He went to see my exhibition of batiks which in 1982 were shown in three Oxford Colleges. He was interested in my process of creating art and I agreed to be interviewed. I was interested to hear what he thought about my work and this is what he said: *"One thing that has struck me about your work since I first saw it, and that is that people are never far away from it. The human figure is always coming in, or is on the point of doing so."* He also responded to the abstract side of my paintings saying, *"An art that has no secrets can only appeal to those who have no secrets of their own. Secrets however, may not be quite the right word here,* for, *inaccessible though it may often seem, Margaret Bialokoz Smith's work is not preoccupied with a private world of inner fantasy. Rather it is characterised by an imaginative exploration of universal themes to which all of us can, in his or her own way respond nor is this an otherworldly art; there is nothing ascetic in the sheer pleasure to be got from these sensuously rhythmic forms and instinctive harmonies of colour and texture."*

The third exhibition, this time in Henley was well received and an anonymous reviewer wrote *"Despite their simplicity, they have a spiritual quality which is both soothing and exhilarating – they speak of new beginnings, harmony, peace, and the oldest of all emotions, love."*

Each year in May I went to a concert in Dorchester Abbey. This splendid mediaeval abbey has excellent acoustics and for me it is a spiritual place which I love to visit. This time I was going with two friends but at the last moment, one could not come and I was hoping to sell the spare ticket at the door, before the concert.

I was lucky, there was a buyer and being in a positive frame of mind, I sold it for a few pounds less than was its price. The friend I went with was a glamorous lady who I knew was interested in meeting nice men. The man who bought my ticket looked like an academic with bright eyes and a cheerful expression. Since the seats were not numbered, I ensured that he sat next to my friend. The only irritating thing was this man's spectacles case which was extremely noisy every time he put his glasses away after reading the programme. This clanging noise was most irritating. During the interval, while we walked the grounds of the abbey, he approached us and with a charming smile announced that since I sold him the ticket for such low price, would we accept his invitation to the pub for a drink after the performance. We readily accepted this invitation and as soon as the performance finished walked across the road to the famous St George Pub. The small space so typical in the old inns, meant that we had to stand with our drinks much too close terrified of having the drinks knocked over and spilled on our clothes. The conversation flowed and we discovered that he was a fellow of St Cross College. I told him that my first husband George was a founder member of that college and that I still have connections with it although my second husband was not connected with the university and that he also died not long ago. He immediately asked me, "*what did you do to them?*" I couldn't help

The Musicians, *drawing, triptych*

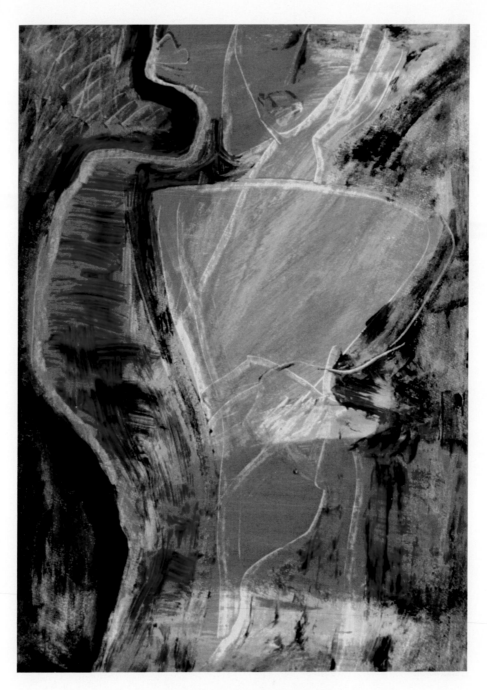

Painting in St Cross College collection

laughing at his response while my friend was visibly shocked. He also told us that he was singing in the Bach Choir and would we like to go to the next concert at the Sheldonian Theatre. I already had a ticket to that concert and so knew that we would meet there. What I did not know at that point was that this chance meeting was going to be the beginning of a special, loving relationship which would last for the next 25 years.

At the beginning of June a letter arrived from my parents, one from my mother and the second one from my father. They expressed longing for our visit and asked for a few objects, like the toilet paper, not available at the time. My mother wrote about the pope's visit to his native country and the joy which prevailed every-where. Most important for her was his message of hope which every Christian should remember. She subsequently wrote an ode in his memory. It was truly inspired full of love, happiness and reflection. My father's reflection on the pope's visit was that of a scientist with a visionary mind who listening to the pope's homilies saw a missed opportunity to teach people to live an honest life infused with crea-tive energy. He wished that hard work was the every-day prayer of every Pole. It might get the country out of the constant stagnation and the lack of progress mostly due to the passive ideology promo-ted by the church. He was hoping for a change in the character of the great majority of Poles although he doubted that such trans-formation would ever happen. If he lived now in 2015 and saw the millions of Poles who leave their country to work in the West he would have been truly shocked but at the same time, not surprised. He believed that getting the experience working in another country is an important learning process and benefits personal growth.

The message of hope which my dear mother found so reassuring was not enough in life and it was not going to help her when she was diagnosed with ovarian cancer. No amount of prayer or hope was going to help her, but she might have extended her life if she had agreed to an operation and treatment. I was hoping to persuade her during my visit in the summer. Whilst I was with her, I saw a great change, from a cheerful, positive and dynamic person, she became withdrawn, sad, often deep in thoughts and much diminished in posture. In spite of her deteriorating health, she was very happy once again to have her family around. I did not succeed in persuading her to have an operation but went to consult her doctor who accepted my mother's decision and understood why she wanted to avoid hospital and chose to stay at home. My cousin Wicek and my sister were with her at the last stage of her life when even the morphine was not giving her respite from pain. Wicek had to carry her to the bathroom when she was no longer able to walk.

I returned home in great distress in the knowledge that I might not see her again. I was in the middle of teaching when the news of her death reached me and my students showed great sympathy seeing me in tears. In spite of their great differences, my parents were very close and my father hoped that he would die before my mother. He lived alone for another ten years being helped by Wicek and his son who kept my father's flat in order.

In spite of my insistence, he never agreed to have a helper who would cook and wash.

The kind neighbours treated him to an occasional meal and he spent most of his time writing and reviewing scientific papers sent to him by his colleagues from abroad.

My parents' 50th wedding anniversary, 1985

Lots of his writing was done whilst sitting in the sun on the balcony where he often fell asleep with the purring, warming cat, Puss, on his lap. Time was of no consequence and mealtime forgotten. Although he was the food specialist and great scientist, he was not able to cook and often went hungry. On Sundays, dear friends the Kwiatkowski came with some excellent food which he greatly appreciated. In spite of his loneliness his spirit remained good and he made trips to his friends in Germany and visited us in Oxford. On one such visit, I had a surprise when waiting at Heathrow for his arrival I saw him approaching on the arm of a stewardess. He had in his hand just two plastic bags bulging with things. No other luggage! No change of clothing!

No pyjamas either! However, he brought gifts and writing material. Luckily our friend Kemble Croft was also very tall and I was able to borrow from him a pair of pyjamas. His visits to us were always full of joy and laughter. He was the most accommodating visitor showing appreciation and positive feedback on the food presented at each meal. Sometimes, my sister joined us and lots of wine flowed, keeping us in good frame of mind.

When Oxford was twinned with Bonn, a cultural contact was made between the artists of both cities. Oxford Artist Group was invited to exhibit in the prestigious Kunstleforum, all of us were very busy preparing our work for the show.

I had no doubt that the work I wished to send there would have to depict the experiences and memories of the horrors of the Second World War. I was preparing a triptych which combined painting, drawing and photographic images all composed on three separate surfaces to be exhibited side by side, making a whole. I was not able to go to Bonn due to my teaching commitments and I had no feedback about my work. For me these paintings were a cleansing process of memories with which I wished to say that I cannot forget the war, and what it did to the whole of the Polish nation.

KÜNSTLERFORUM

OUTSIDERS

AN EXHIBITION BY ARTISTS FROM
OTHER COUNTRIES LIVING IN BONN
TOGETHER WITH ARTISTS FROM
OXFORD
5. 9. — 25. 9. 1987
BONN 1/HOCHSTADENRING 22

Two of the three images for the exhibition in Bonn

The same year, an opportunity arrived to take part in the Artists in School Programme and since I was very fond of children I took part in it. I had to plan a project suitable for a particular age group. In my first placement I was with teenagers in Bicester Community College. It was going well and the young people were interested and applied themselves, accept for one boy who seem to have problem in understanding and constantly copied his neighbour's work. I decided to give him as much attention as was possible and I could see that this was very helpful to him. I became concerned and talked to the head teacher who told me that this youngster needed one-to-one contact with the teaching staff but in a class of over 30 pupils it was impossible. It meant that he would go through the school and not achieve much. In Poland the children who were slow had to repeat the year and in this way had a chance to achieve the necessary results. My second residency was in a primary school in Oxford. The open plan layout of the school meant that the groups of children were separated from each other only by some shelving units and could hear what was happening in the next group. If there was a disruptive child it affected many other children. I had in my group one such girl who was quite obviously a very disturbed child. The session which I planned for them consisted of using their hands and feet to paint on a very long piece of paper. When I talked about it to the very attentive group of youngsters, the girl was unable to sit still, jumped up and down, on top of the tables making sure that everybody took notice of her and wanted to be the centre of attention. When the time came to paint, she was so impossible that I smacked her bottom to which she reacted immediately. She became quiet, after the initial shock and joined everybody. One little Japanese girl refused to put her hands and feet in paint because getting dirty was not something her mother would approve of. I had to report to the headmistress that I smacked the disruptive child and hopefully find out more about her. If I was employed by the school I could have been fired for smacking a child but since I was not, I was risking nothing. I was told that this exceptionally tall girl was brought up by a single mother who had many unhappy relationships with different men. There was much aggression which the girl witnessed and when asked she repeatedly said that she did not want to be a girl. Her behaviour was thus explained although nobody knew how to help her. I enjoyed my sessions at the schools although it was time when I suffered from tremendous migraines.

The stressful situations exasperated it but I had no time to deal with it except by taking painkillers. It did not stop me from producing some art on the subject of family and children. I made one of my favourite etchings "The Family" and paintings depicting children. The experience of being once again with children was inspirational.

R. W. Emerson, nineteenth-century philosopher and poet in one of his writings "*The Conduct of Life*", affirms the importance of the individual and amongst wise thoughts said *"For everything you have missed, you have gained something else; and for everything you gain, you lose something."* So it was in my life. The man I met in Dorchester at a concert in May 1987, and later again at the concert of the Bach Choir, was Dr Godfrey Tyler, an agricultural economist and the fellow of St Cross College. He loved nature, supported various national schemes concerned with the preservation of the countryside, loved music and for years sang in the Bach Choir. As a young boy he sung in choirs with his mother whilst the father was an organist. Apart from music, sailing was also one of his passions. His first boat was a small one which he towed to the Broads or to the sea. By the time we met he had a big, 25-footer and a glamorous girlfriend who sailed with him at sea round the Chichester area. During Open Studios, Godfrey visited me with his glamorous girlfriend who was charming. At some point during their visit, she took me to the side and said, *"you are right for him, you can have him"*. I was astonished indeed at her remark and taken aback.

I liked Godfrey, his lovely sense of humour, positive approach to life and cheerful disposition. We shared the love of nature, music and sailing which I had not done since 1957 when for the last time I sailed with my father. Godfrey had no affinity with contemporary art but liked the colours in my painting – so he assured me. Many years earlier, he was married to a painter who was an accomplished traditional artist. They had three daughters and when they were still very young, his wife decided to leave him and take the children to Canterbury where her parents lived. He had no option but agree to divorce her and for years suffered greatly knowing what the impact it would have on the lives of his girls. Godfrey had to go through the courts to achieve the rights of access to his children. He also had to support them financially until they finished higher education.

With Godfrey at Christmas

He bought a large uninteresting house in the village of Wendlebury where his girls came to visit him for a time agreed by the
courts. His mother and her sister could also visit and prepare food
for everybody. A string of girlfriends always glamorous were a sort
of consolation for Godfrey who genuinely loved being with women.
When I met his daughters years later, I could not but wonder how
different their lives would have been, brought up with the father's
input into their education within the Oxford's culture.

The more I got to know Godfrey, the more I liked him and I
appreciated his interest in my professional life. We met at weekends
to walk in the countryside following many paths crisscrossing the
fields and giving the public the right of way. We went to concerts
and dinners at St Cross College. He willingly transported my art to
exhibitions and enjoyed the socialising with the crowd of artists.
The Hill Gallery in Hampstead was interested in my art and invited
me to exhibit there. They came to collect all my work and hung it
themselves. The large collection of etchings was to be shown in a
browser. It was a kind of retrospective exhibition and although the
paintings belonged to different periods, they looked well together.

Unfortunately, I did not know that the owners of the gallery were not honest the fact I discovered after the show. They returned my paintings but kept all work on paper. Alexander came to the rescue when with his friend – both tall and strong guys – went to the gallery demanding the return of my work. I can imagine that the small in stature owners must have been rather worried by the confrontation and without much ado, all my prints were handed over to the boys. Subsequently I discovered that the gallery owners went to Poland, visited the studios of well-known artists and bought their art for a few dollars. It was a great investment for them and the artists, were happy to be paid in dollars which when exchanged on the black market gave good return.

The day when Godfrey invited me to sail on his big yacht was a memorable one. I couldn't even compare it with my father's boat where we slept on the hard floor, which was covered with smelling wild boars' skins. Of course, I was always looking forward to our expeditions on the small sailing boat *Strybog*.

The big yacht of Godfrey's was a luxury with a toilet, stove and sitting area which at night converted into comfortable beds. Lots of hidden storage meant that nothing would fly around when the boat

Godfrey Tyler with his boat, Dolly Kedge 2

heeled. It was a twin-keeled boat which meant that at low tide it rested in an upright position. If the weather was pleasant and the tide was high Godfrey loved getting out of the marina in Emsworth and sail in the Solent. The weather was often unpredictable and some funny adventures awaited me like the ones I had while sailing with my father. Lessons are always to be learned. One should never drop an anchor for the night at sea but rather in the marina or a sheltered estuary. We made once such mistake when the forecast was for good, calm weather overnight. The sunset was blissful, the sea calm, the weather balmy and we dropped the anchor for the night outside Bembridge, the Isle of Wight. During the night, the weather changed and a very strong wind was tossing the boat non-stop. It was so rough that even standing upright in the cabin was impossible. On top of that, both of us were constantly seasick. Somehow, we got out of the cabin, wrapped ourselves up in blankets and stayed on the deck till the weather changed and the sun came out.

I loved cooking on the boat and making pancakes was my favourite. I usually started cooking when Godfrey was slowly getting the boat into some sort of marina and by the time the anchor was down or we were attached to a buoy, we were ready for a pre-dinner drink followed by pancakes and fruit. After the first weekend at sea, I produced a big monoprint of the sea scene for Godfrey's office. It was the only painting which I have done of the sea in spite of sailing for so many years. For me nature is so perfect, the sea so complete that there was no point in making portraits of it. Sometimes I painted an interpretation of the natural world as I felt and experienced it but it did not happen often.

There were times when I did not wish to walk or sail but wanted to paint, however, I never had courage to say it to Godfrey because it would have upset him greatly. All my life, I disliked problematic confrontations and for the sake of peace gave in. Emerson was right that by gaining something we have to lose something else!

12. Poets, Art, Radom

Art always tells part of the truth, and this part is profound because in describing human joy and suffering, artists record and transmit profound aspects of human experience.

Edward Bond

The tyranny of the Soviet communism imposed on Poland after the war continued until the summer of 1980. The widespread discontent brought strikes in industries and shipyards. In the Gdansk shipyard the workers established an independent trade union Solidarnosc [Solidarity]. The visit of the Polish pope, John Paul II, to Poland gave the nation a new sense of optimism in the knowledge that they now had a true spokesman in international affairs. *"IF A POLE COULD BECOME POPE THEN PERHAPS POLAND COULD BECOME FREE."* Discontent, strikes, arrests, imprisonment of the activists were the normal occurrence. Repercussions from the communist government could not stop the hard and determined fight for freedom. On the 4th June 1989 came the final victory and the end of communism in Poland but the last Russian troops left in 1993.

Around 10 million Poles live in the West. These emigrants kept constantly in touch with their friends and families. The parcels with food products, objects of all sorts, discarded equipment from hospitals were sent in transports to Poland.

Our visits to Poland each year, sometimes twice a year were always combined with joy and sadness. As foreigners, we had to register with the police within 48 hours of our arrival. We were obliged to pay a certain sum of dollars for each day of our stay in the country.

The inevitable dualism, the polarity is part of our life and exists in everything: spirit–matter, man–woman, subjective–objective, odd –even, good–bad. In one country life is peaceful, in another a raging war. Can a happy equilibrium exist anywhere or are we as humanity doomed to eternal struggle?

During one Art Week, Open Studios, I had a visit from a well-known poet, Elizabeth Jennings. She particularly liked my recent collection of etchings. She told me that my work is unique and wondered if I would like to collaborate with her in production of the next volume of her poetry. This was an exciting suggestion from the poet whose work I liked very much. There was a great depth of feelings and wonderful rich vision in her poems. She was going to talk to the publisher who unfortunately was not interested in our collaboration. We were both disappointed, but the editors, like the art curators are the decision makers regardless of what the writer or an artist wishes.

Open Studio
1997, Oxford

Elizabeth wrote most of her poems by hand, sitting in her bed or in a favourite place of a particular pub where she was well known. She walked there carrying two heavy plastic bags, wearing a very old worn-out coat and a knitted hat. She always looked neglected and nobody could have imagined that this woman was one of the best

English poets. When she had a pile of handwritten poems, she gave them to her friend, Ruzena Stanley, a sweet little woman, who patiently deciphered Elizabeth's writing and typed it out for the publishers. Ruzena told me that she was always concerned about Elizabeth's wellbeing because she did not, or rather was not interested in looking after herself. She lived in a small flat, just big enough to accommodate the collection of eight dollhouses – her great hobby. Priscilla Tolkien, a close friend of Elizabeth organised financial support for the poet through the Tolkien Trust.

Peter Levi wrote about her poetry thus: "*She conveys a sense of something hidden but powerfully alive in her: she may be the last poet of what used to be called the soul. She is one of a few living poets one could not do without.*"

After Elizabeth died, her trusty friend and secretary, Ruzena, became lost and very depressed. Priscilla who is the kindest person under the sun, suggested that perhaps a trip to Prague, Ruzena's city of childhood, might be the right thing to do. She invited Ruzena and together, they arrived at Heathrow to take the flight at which point Ruzena suffered what one might call a panic attack. She was suddenly aware of having to face the memories of the horrors of the war in which all her family was gassed in Auschwitz. Aware of the drama ahead, she was not mentally ready and the trip was cancelled.

Soon after, she ended her life and at last was free of suffering.

This is the last verse from Elizabeth's poem "DUST"

> *A place for vision, a hope*
> *That reaches beyond the stars,*
> *Conjures and pauses the seas,*
> *Dust discovers our own*
> *Proud, torn destinies.*
> *Yes, we are dust to the bone.*

One of a thousand photographs of flowers

The meeting of special and unique people is always a privilege and a source of inspiration. Each person is unique and for me always extremely interesting because each life is a different story, never boring and always intriguing.

1992 was a busy year, with two important exhibitions. As a result of the first one in Cambridge, I met another poet, Edward Bond, who is an outstanding, internationally known, playwright. The Cambridge Exhibition at Heffers Gallery consisted of 40 paintings and drawings. The excellent natural lighting enhanced the colours in my work. It was well hung and well received by the public. I feel that there is need for introducing an exhibition of contemporary art and this is what I said in the introduction to my show:

"I feel, that there are parallels between painting, poetry and music. They all give us freedom of interpretation, and allow for the creation of new ideas and, sometimes, new vision. To me, every painting is a new story, always! A composer does not describe his musical compositions, but allows the listener to respond to it in his own way. The novelty of the work requires willingness and openness on the part of the listener, and it applies also to viewing a contemporary work of art."

Edward Bond and his wife Elisabeth, enjoyed the exhibition, bought a painting called "Figures in Space", and at a later time, came to my studio to buy another painting. The following is what he said about my paintings: *"There is darkness in the pictures, but chiefly there is hope and a sort of effulgent affirmation. It must give you pleasure to know that there must be many places which are made more human by the presence of your vision."* When they bought the painting, "Feminine Encounters", he wrote: *"One really has not just to look at it, or even reflect on it, – but one has to look into it. It is a profound picture. You probably need years to get to know it."*

At Christmas time, I receive, each year from Edward and his wife, a poem with good wishes for the year to come. It is a most welcomed gift.

My second exhibition took place in the Museum of Contemporary Art in Radom, Poland. The city is situated two-hour train journey from Warsaw. The choice of work was mine. I took all my work in the same, very large portfolio, with which I travelled to Karachi. The beginning of my journey was in Warsaw, where I stayed with my very dear uncle Ric and aunt Zula, my mother's family. From there, I took the train to Radom. In Poland, I usually travel in the first class, to avoid crowded compartments. This time it was a mistake because I was isolated, sitting alone. In fact, all the compartments of the first class wagon, were empty. I was told some time ago, that particularly on that stretch of the line, robberies occur. The train stops at every station of which there are many making it easy to hop on and off, having done the dirty job on a passenger. I did not have to wait long before a rough looking couple walked into my compartment. They watched me intently, never exchanging a single word. I was relieved, when the conductor walked in to check the tickets. He completely ignored the other passengers and did not ask for their tickets. I was rather worried, but decided to play a sort of game. To start with, I got up to show my height, stretched in different ways. Next, I opened my big portfolio and proceeded examining with great care, each of my 40 pieces of art. The couple just went on looking at me very intently. When I finished examining my pictures, I went on fiddling with this big portfolio, making as much commotion as possible. The result was what I was hoping for, the couple nodded to each other and left. I could now relax, till the train reached Radom where I was met by my hosts. Their reaction to my tale was that I most probably avoided being robbed, because I was so tall and made so much commotion and above all had my hand bag attached to me all the time. If I was a little dainty

All Around Me, *drawing*

lady, I would have arrived in Radom without my handbag and a nervous wreck!

The Museum of Contemporary Art in Radom is situated in an old building, in the centre of the town's pretty market square, the only restored part of town. Otherwise, the town is very bleak with dozens of identical blocks of flats. The old houses behind the restored market centre, are in a terrible state of war time damage.

The high blocks of flats often have lifts out of order. I have witnessed a man in a wheelchair being hoisted out of a window, high up, held by ropes with pulleys, slowly lowered down to the ground. My host Z. Kaminski, lived with his wife and four children in one such block of flats. They had two rooms, kitchen and a minute bathroom. They never once complained, were most welcoming and content.

I was staying in a theatre hostel, from which it was a short walk to the museum where over the next few days, I was involved in putting up my exhibition. Many willing helpers, made the job less exhausting. The exhibition was called "Wydarzenia–Happenings", and all the texts for the public were produced by the museum in Polish and English. All my pictures were the result of two years of concentrated work and were meant to be exhibited together. Some images were painted on recycled, handmade paper, on which I used a variety of techniques, drawing, painting and often printing to achieve the required result. The opening of the exhibition was well attended and I was delighted that two of my college friends came from Gdansk.

Aniela Kita, my oldest friend, by now a well-known painter and stained glass designer produced, years earlier, stained glass windows for the biggest church in Radom. It was a lovely diversion to go and look at this splendid collection of geometrical designs which made the whole interior of the very modern church sing with warm light and colour.

The churches in Poland are very wealthy, often monumental, in spite of the poor and neglected housing all around them. The existence of the museum in Radom was the result of hard work of a few very energetic individuals who had the ambition to create a cultural centre in otherwise a bleak industrial town. A group of good artists with tough attitudes and determination as well as contacts within the local bureaucracy must have been behind the creation of an artistic venue, which the museum became.

I was most impressed and happy to add some of my work to their permanent collection of contemporary art. Z. Kamienski reviewed my exhibition with these words: *"Malgorzata's paintings express her own world of colours and lines. When the impact of events is overwhelming, the abstractions are suddenly transformed – with the aid of powerful brush stroke – into a human form, a tree, a bird."*

Summer came with an invitation from Godfrey to accompany him on a walking holiday in the Austrian Alps. My ever supportive children, bought me a pair of walking boots and a backpack. My only serious walking went back to my teens, when with Jola, my archaeologist friend, we walked in the southern Poland. The rolling hills and villages, scattered amongst forests, were my first experience in serious walking over many days.

Walking down the hill for an hour caused the leg muscles to object and cause cramps.

To remedy the discomfort, we proceeded to walk up again for a few minutes.

We never knew where we would find a bed for the night. This was a real countryside, without hostels or tourist accommodation. Each village we came to, surprised us with different craft produced there, mostly by the women. The lace making was the speciality of that particular region. Women sat outside their huts and made lace of all sorts. I bought a lace collar which, for many years, I attached to an evening dress. When we walked into a village, there was always a welcoming sour milk drink and a sleep in a barn, if no other space was available. Women of these villages, had a curious

The Mountains, *acrylic on paper*

habit of singing at the top of their voices, across the valleys, to communicate with each other. A substitute for the telephones! On Sundays, women and children, in every village, dressed in their traditional colourful costumes and walked to the church, quite a distant away.

I was telling Godfrey all about these past memories, when we walked the beautiful treks of the Alps where the meadows were full of scent and colour, and the distant peaks covered in snow. Our hotel was delightful, with a balcony full of a rampant display of vivid pelargoniums. The village, called Alpbach, is 1000m above the sea level and the air is incredibly fresh and sharp. In rain, the scent of the fields becomes accentuated. The view from our balcony went through many changes, depending on the time of day, and the weather. The intensity of light changed the colours of the landscape. The clouds sometimes enveloped the valley, usually for a short time. The weather changes in the mountains are the same as at sea. On the day when the sun shone and everything looked idyllic, we went in a cable car, high up towards the snow and while sitting suspended in the chairs, moving slowly up, a snowstorm descended and suddenly it was winter!

It was worth getting cold because when we arrived at the top, we were a few yards from the entrance to a glacier. The light inside it was amazingly diffused, almost as if the sunlight has been trapped in it and, in a strange way, excluded all shadows. It seemed to filter through the ice, from every direction. After the first three days of intense walking, our muscles were in need of rest, and we took the bus to a delightful old town of Rattenberg am Inn. In that small town, every house was different in its design and colour. Many gift shops offered local crafts of wooden objects and woven garments, table cloths and napkins. Tyrol has its specific pattern in designs, but there is no regional variety which is in the Polish folklore. My first experience of high mountains had an inspirational impact and I spent evenings making small format paintings, which were lying around our room to dry. This must have been reported by the chambermaid to the owner, who asked me if I would sell him some to put up in the hotel, where the usual genteel water colours adorned the walls. I was delighted to oblige, and hope that they are still on the walls of that delightful place where we had our first, memorable walking holidays.

Godfrey was a lovely companion, a cheerful and caring man. He was sensitive and understanding. When I told him how much I missed my mother, he told me that he was also very close to his own mother, whom he adored. Dorothy was besotted with her only son who, in return, lavished much care on his mother. We always wrote cards to Dorothy and visited her often. I missed the time when I could tell my mother about the beauty of nature and the mountains all around us. She instilled in me the appreciation of the natural world, changing through the seasons. In spring, during our walks, she picked an interesting branch and placed it in the middle of the table for the family to watch the slow waking up of the buds in the warmth of the room. She told me a quote from a Hindu culture, "*If you have a rupee, buy a piece of bread to feed the body* and a *flower to feed the soul*". That flower was to be placed on the bedside table, so that in the morning, it would be the first thing one could look at. This was the oriental philosophy, a follow up of the Hindu one. My waking time is for thinking about the dream I had and the things to be done on that particular day. My dreams are very important to me. Every night I enter a world of very colourful pictures and events, which I like to ponder over, when I wake up, if time allows for such a luxury! When I dream about a particular friend, I ring up that friend to find out if all is well. It is not a superstition but a chance to make contact. I once had a dream about my close friend, Sally Croft, in which she showed me round the new house she and her husband had moved to. When I rang her up to tell her about the dream, I discovered that they were indeed moving to a new house, soon but it was not like the one in my dream but rather dilapidated, neglected for years, old cottage. She and her husband moved every few years to a new house which they always redesigned and made into the most delightful home.

Each week, Radio 3 has a couple of hours devoted to a particular composer. One such week was devoted to a Polish twentieth-century composer – Szymanowski. He composed in 1926 Stabat Mater, which is a religious composition of great simplicity and emotional charge. During his lifetime, he was rarely played and suffered financial hardship. His music, inspired two composers – H. Gorecki and Arvo Part. His Stabat Mater also inspired my two paintings, subject of which were "angels".

When an invitation came from the art centre in Knigton Powys, in Wales, Godfrey was delighted to take me there to take part in the exhibition and the weekend workshop.

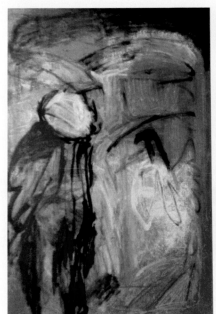

Painting on the subject of angels

The subject of the exhibition and discussions was angels. We combined it with long walks, in the beautiful countryside round Knigton Powys. The guest speaker at the conference was James Roose-Evans, the author of *Passages of the Soul*. The book is about the spiritual journey in which rituals play a key role. Kathleen Rain, the poet, said the following about his book: "*He speaks to this time and to a generation for whom ritual is not something to be discarded but to be discovered.*" For me walking in the landscape belongs to the spiritual ritual and so does the creation of my art. The two pictures of angels for the exhibition allowed for interpretation of the subject.

The stories of angels are part of many cultures and religions. There are people amongst us who experience and see the world of angels. Are these mystical experiences a product of our fantasy? Some think so, but I do not. As a child, I had a dream of being in a cellar, very dank where water was seeping through the walls. I was wearing a thin, white nightie and I was hungry and frightened. Suddenly, a light appeared and in it an angel like figure handing me a piece of bread. At that point, the dream ended and left me full of wonder.

I never told anybody about it, I was afraid of being laughed at. Although I live in a material dimension, a few powerful experiences of the spiritual kind formed my belief in the supernatural. Perhaps our brains are not capable of comprehending the possibilities of other dimensions, beyond our reality. The experiences of our childhood stay with us and form the basis of our beliefs and become part of our personality. During the few critical moments in my life in situations when I needed help, calling on my angels, I mysteriously received it. Each time it happened I was left in awe and full of gratitude. Perhaps, in spite of all advanced available technology, we will never discover the secret of the supernatural and its mystical dimension.

Music, like nature, is important to me and my life would be very impoverished if I had to live without experiencing its beneficial influence. The contemporary composer Andrzej Panufnik escaped from Poland after the war and came to England where he established himself as a composer of great merit. For me the particular compositions, Symphonia Sacra and Symhonia Rustica, became the great inspiration for an etching which I dedicated to these two symphonies. Andrzej Panufnik liked my vision of his work produced as an etching and was pleased to receive the gift of the print.

Music often inspired my art and after attending many concerts with Godfrey, I produced a series of drawings and paintings on the subject. A few years later, I showed the collection of work on the subject of music at a Chelsea Gallery. When a girl from Thailand bought a picture, I was happy to have a sample of my artistic output in yet another country.

The events in my life and the historical time in which I live, are inspiring my artistic work. The memories of war, motherhood,

Family on the way to a wedding in Victoria, Canada
(left to right) Bianca, Barbara, David and Christopher

raising the family, the cultures I touched on during my travels, the
people I love and the environment in which I happen to live at the
given time, all are reflected in my art as are the devastations of
which humanity is capable. The techniques which I use change as
does the style, depending on the subject I am involved with at the
time. Some work belongs to the long gone past – the old work,
some is new and some belong to the future. Our life is like a balanc-
ing act and applies to our existence and its creative processes.

My children are now fully independent adults, having achieved
their professional aims and still very much involved with sport.
Alex continues playing volleyball, while Barbara, now living on the
east coast of Canada, gave up volleyball and the triathlon and continues biking. She met the love of her life – Dave Mcleod, also a
biker, and I am reassured seeing her very happy in her work and her
personal life. Alex met a beautiful German girl, Frauke, at a
volleyball tournament and fell in love. For a year, she was studying
in Oxford – European Business Studies and was also playing

Frauke and Alex's wedding, September 1995

volleyball in her spare time. In 1990 they married in Oxford. This was a lovely celebration and a gathering of extremely good looking, very tall sports people. For me it was also a special time, meeting her very nice family. I wished I spoke German to be able to communicate with them. At school, we had compulsory Russian language which is useless to me. German is a difficult language and would require an immense amount of time to acquire it. With age, memory is not as ready to retain new knowledge and the new language. I joined a learning group in hope of acquiring some knowledge of German language to no avail. Every lesson was as if it was a complete novelty, as if I was starting again. I soon gave up!

13. Artist Friends, Father

Each of us is the destiny of the universe...
Edward Bond

My parents' participation in the upbringing of my children was greatly appreciated by myself and enjoyed by my children when, almost every summer since the age of eight and nine, they travelled often alone to stay with them in Sopot. When my term ended, I joined them and sometimes my sister came also with her husband Peter. If the weather was kind, much of the day was spent on the beach swimming and playing ballgames. My mother was determined to harden the children and insisted that they must swim even on a cold and wet day! It was her great determination to make the children strong and ready to return to school in an excellent state of health. Unfortunately, in those distant years, the Baltic Sea was polluted by the shipping. The Russian ships emptied their refuse into this area of the Baltic Bay. In spite of some tummy upsets the children survived. I often wondered how my parents managed to feed all their guests with the constant food shortages. I often found myself fuming with fury at the situations which I could not understand while my parents had to deal with them on a daily basis. My father's saying *"It could be worse"* was heard in our family a lot. The two important aspects of their life was the group of friends who supported each other and the beautiful nature within walking distance which nourished their souls. The only real freedom is that of the mind. Strength has to come from within. Religious belief is another source of strength.

*Relative Images
exhibition with
Paddy Bowler,
Jean Blumberg
and Judith Roberts*

Mandela talked about it in his autobiography. In spite of years in prison, in the end he was victorious and the freedom of his mind was his biggest source of strength.

Socialising with a group of like-minded friends is one of the most enjoyable activities in our life. Like my parents, I had a group of artist friends. We met, talked, had parties and exhibited our art together. All of them had families to look after, demanding academic husbands and, in between, managed to have that great freedom of creativity. The four of us, Jean Blumberg, Paddy Bowler and Judith Roberts and I, had an exhibition in Wolfson College. We called it "RELATIVE IMAGES" since our work was very different. We had three rooms in which during term time, tutorials and meetings took place which meant that our works would be seen by a lot of people. Some of my pictures had frames with glass and the reflections from the huge windows on the opposite wall were creating another picture on the surface of the glass. An hour before the opening, I had to take my big frames down to remove all the glass plates. It worked well although the surface of the picture was fragile consisting of layers of paper. We invited our friends for the opening and the party and the show were a great success. Barry Blumberg, Jean's husband was at that time the master of Balliol College and a famous medical man who discovered the Hepatitis B virus and received, in 1976, the Nobel Prize in medicine.

He was a lively, modest man with a splendid sense of humour.

Jean was like him, very friendly and positive woman who produced big canvases of immense colourful energy.

Paddy Bowler was a very talented printmaker whose work consisted of collages and etchings of complex geometric patterns inspired often by oriental textiles and ancient letter forms. She was bringing up two sons with the husband, a scholar of a rather solemn kind! We all loved Paddy whose laughter was catching, while we avoided her husband. Paddy's dormant cancer after years of remission, suddenly came back and she died unexpectedly. Her husband refused to tell her friends about the funeral so we were deprived of saying the last farewell. We decided to hold a silent vigil in the chapel of Merton College with which she was connected. Years later a group of her printmaker friends insisted on getting access to Paddy's work, to make a retrospective exhibition in the Christ Church Gallery. The husband and the charming two sons joined us at the opening of the show. My third friend, Judith Roberts by profession was a marriage guidance counsellor who later studied fine art at Southampton. Her work had great elegance and was immaculately executed. Her husband was an acting Master of Merton College when we met. Both of them were party loving people and their dinners were always a time for meeting unusual guests. Godfrey and I met there the famous Irish pianist, Barry Douglas.

The following day, he was playing at a concert to which we all went. One of his favourite composers was Brahms with whose music he had great affinity. He describes it in following words: "*it is a delicate interweaving of the very essence of our existence: I treasure every phrase!*" Douglas plays with massive power and his interpretation always has a visionary quality. He is truly a powerful performer. At one concert, his incredibly powerful and almost violent performance made me wonder if the instrument could survive without being damaged. I always loved piano as an instrument of great richness of tone and endless possibilities in expression. I was delighted when Barbara expressed a wish to learn and I bought an upright piano from a young woman who was told by her husband that the piano should go because she will have no time to play. I paid £20 and the woman was in tears when the piano was loaded on a truck. Barbara was true to her words and went on learning till she passed grade 6. When my father visited us, he sat at the piano and after a 60-year gap, he still remembered a lovely old tune.

In his youth, every child had to learn to play and he remembered the hours of practice to achieve a good standard and be able to entertain the family and friends.

Oxford Craft Guild had many talented members and for a time I had joined it to participate in their exhibitions. I was the only artist working in batik. The texture of batik is characteristically crazed and is similar to the surface of raku pottery which I first saw in Edith Holt's pots. She showed me the process of producing a raku pot. What I particularly loved was the element of surprise when you take the pot out of hot ashes and submerge it in cold water. That drastic temperature reduction cracks the glaze of the pot in unexpected way. This element of surprise is similar to the moment when you produce a print. Edith and I had an exhibition together. Her pots and lamps with hand painted lampshades went well with my prints and paintings. A few months prior to our exhibition I had an idea of producing a small edition of prints in combination with excerpts from poems which particularly had meaning for me. Page one had a verse from the

*Raku figure on wood,
my experiment*

Bible, page two, William Wordsworth's *Tintern Abbey*, page three, William Blake's *William Bond*, page four, Rabindranath Tagore's *Fruit Gathering*, page five, T. S. Elliot's *The Rock*, page six, Goethe's *The Eye has Light...*, page seven, Kathleen Raine's *Eudaimon*, page eight, Elizabeth Jennings's *One Flesh*. I spent much time designing each page, typesetting by hand each letter and using an etched plates to create the image. This project was important for me in order to consolidate ideas which were slowly growing in my mind. I produced an edition of seven copies of the above.

Two other potter friends of mine, Audrey Stockwin and Betty Blandino both produced completely different pots. Audrey's were earthly and strong with minimal decoration whilst Betty's were made by coiling clay. She wrote two books on the history and the technique of making coiled pottery. The surface texture of her pots maintained the characteristic of the clay she used. The variety of shapes and sizes which Betty produced were, from the miniature size of an eggshell to two feet tall shapes of great beauty. I loved the pots of all my friends and exhibited my work with each one. While exhibiting with Audrey in Cambridge, I found a message in the visitor's book from a Japanese girl: "*Your work is wonderful, please bring it to Japan*"! It is always a joy to have a response from the visitors to an exhibition. Edith, Betty and I held an exhibition in the North Wall Arts Centre in Oxford in 2010. The venue was excellent with good lighting and lots of wall space. There was also a theatre which provided for us an additional viewing public. Our works complemented each other. Big wall space meant that I could exhibit my very large paintings. Painting on fabric means that I can fold it up into a small bundle for transport, unfold and thread at the top and bottom with wooden batons for hanging. Putting up an exhibition is always time consuming but measuring up the space of the walls and making a maquette of the interior is very helpful. Alexander has an amazing skill in putting up my exhibitions. Twice, he astonished me in placing over 30 paintings on the walls in the exact order in a few hours while it would have taken me the whole day. This

Stage 1 of batik painting of Oxford (left)
and finished batik (above)

exhibition at the North Wall Arts Centre was Betty's last one, she developed a brain tumour which could not be treated. She could never make another pot and her friends cherish the ones they have. Betty was the energetic and encouraging friend and a famous potter who was always full of future plans and knew how to promote her work. Her funeral took place in a Roman Catholic Church. Participation in the service by the friends and family members was out of question. There is a saying that the difference between the RC church and the Anglican is that the first one expects to be served by the parishioners while the second one is in the service to its parishioners! I experienced the same aloofness of the parish priests in Poland when my father died. I had asked the priest to read particular passages from the Bible during the funeral service for my father. He flatly refused. I discovered subsequently that the coffin was also not allowed in the church during the service. I was so shocked that I refused to attend the service and stayed with the coffin which was placed in another building a long distance away. At the end of the service all the people who attended it, probably over a hundred, walked up the hill to the gravesite. The coffin was placed on a cart and two black horses had to take it up the hill through the wooded cemetery. My father was a tall man but the coffin delivered to the undertaker was too small.

I was informed when visiting him laid out, that my father's feet had to be cut off to fit him in the coffin. The big moustache which he never had in his life, made him look dreadful and the ugly white lace trimming all around the edge of the coffin was deplorable. I had more surprises at the gravesite! Completely unknown to the family, the university organised their own spectacle. There were loud-speakers installed on the pine trees which grow all around the cemetery and the marine orchestra was to play the hymns and a funeral march. The revolting priest was the centre of this theatrical performance when for at least 20 minutes he went on reciting the litany to all the known saints. The crowd of mourners stood in silence in bitter cold. One of my father's colleagues was in his nineties and came to say his farewell from a distant city of Poznan. I felt so sorry for this dear old man who had to stand for well over an hour and listen to the various speeches by dignitaries and scientists. When asked if I wished to say something I refused. After 25 years of being kept out of his valuable scientific work, the university expressed regret at his grave! How could I have any respect for them? I wished that this theatrical performance was a bad dream from which I would wake up. After the funeral, the family went their way and was not invited to the reception which took place at the university. I had absolutely no say about the procedure of my father's funeral which should have been our way of saying the last farewell in the magnificent setting of the silent and snow covered forest.

I saw my father for the last time while he was in hospital. I had to wait till my term ended before I was able to leave to be by his bedside. By that time he was unconscious and I sat with him talking about our time when we sailed and reminded him how much he has achieved in his long life of 93 years, always overcoming the obstacles, always positive and moving on! He was in a tiny room and nursing was so unsatisfactory that my cousin employed a nurse to look after him. Our friends insisted that I should leave his bedside, to have some food and return afterwards. Reluctantly, I took their advice, as it happened a bad one! By the time I returned to hospital it was late and the place looked almost deserted. Reaching the second floor, I saw our nurse standing and in tears. Father had died a while ago, but just before, he became conscious and asked her to sing with him the short verse we all know from the fairy tale *Hay Ho, Hey Ho, to work we shall go*. These were his last words.

I missed what would have been a special moment to remember for ever. While I tried to console the nurse, two men came holding a big sack, uncovered my father's body (I saw the awful bedsores) put his body into it and carried it out like a load of coal. I was speechless at the brutality of it all. Before this happened, I had a moment to marvel at the change which took place in his face. He reminded me of the faces of the Egyptian pharaohs.

It was a beautiful head, although it did not seem to resemble my father. And as soon as I got back to my parents flat, I went to my father's study to make some drawings. The room was so full of my father, all his files, the old trusty friend the typewriter, the medals on the wall together with the photos of the eminent colleagues, the tools hanging neatly on the side of the old desk. The room should have been protected as a relic and placed in a museum of humanity as the example of a unique study of a scientist who lived in the communist Poland. The future visitors to such room would have been astonished by the uniqueness and the history of it. I was surrounded by an immense silence and drawings just came out of my feelings which I could not describe in any other way.

My Father Died, *three of six drawings*

When I returned to Oxford, much time was needed for healing and returning to normality of every day. Godfrey, my dear and caring friend, suggested that perhaps a trip to the Alps for cross country skiing might restore my mental balance. It was wintertime and the idea of seeing the lovely scenery in white was appealing. We flew to Switzerland on a small plane from London airport. On the approach to landing at the snow covered airport we heard on the intercom a worrying call, *"we are short, we are short"*, all passengers who were glued to the windows admiring the landscape froze. We landed in a wobble, grateful for avoiding, I guess, skidding? A connecting bus took us to Kandersteg and the old hotel Victoria. The peacefulness and the silence of the snowy landscape was bewildering and I made a big effort not to think about not so distant experiences. I had a lovely surprise that evening when I saw sitting at the next table, one of my students, Kathy and her husband Rey. They love to ski and come to Kandersteg every winter and both are experts in the cross-country skiing. We hired the boots which are attached to incredibly light skis and joined a group of learners. Most of the time, the weather was blissful but one day we saw the savageness of the Alps, a great power of nature like a mighty mountain symphony engulfing everything. One feels very, very small and insignificant in the majesty of the wild nature. We learned how to stay on skis and not to fall down, we ate some traditional, very rich dishes and we enjoyed the company of Kathy and Rey. Following our unexpected meeting, they visited my studio, liked various paintings and drawings which now enrich their home.

Kandersteg, with Godfrey

Decision Making, *1997, acrylic*

14. France, Alps, Halifax

If science is something people do, art is an expression of what they are: a process in nature.

Edward Bond

In every person's life there exists an experience of an immensely powerful sense of soul.

It might be a place protected from the onslaughts of the world made by men or by nature.

For me, one such place was the Yosemite Valley in California and the other the Maeght Foundation in the south of France. The first one is the wonder of nature, wild and unspoiled by men while the second one is creation of husband and wife whose passion for contemporary art found expression in creating a remarkable "living" space for artists.

The buildings were designed to house a large collection of art produced by well-known European artists and the studios a part of the complex to accommodate those who wish to work in the most inspiring environment. I experienced there a great feeling of belonging and felt that my work could hang there happily. The passion of the creative spirit was overwhelming and Godfrey appreciated my elation on that day. We were visiting friends living near Cannes and had time to look at a few art places. The Maeght Foundation was the most interesting one. My favourite Alberto Giacometti, Marc Chagall, Joan Miro and George Braque had their own rooms and many of their sculptures were incorporated into the landscape. Meetings of artists and the many concerts held there were the opportunity to hear experimental jazz music as well as classical and contemporary composers.

The Foundation had its own cinema where documentary, and experimental films of different filmmakers were projected. It was truly a living place for the Arts.

The English art scene is very different. The many galleries are promoting their own groups of artists in order to make money. There are some dishonest curators and I experienced that during my long life of exhibiting. In Hamburg, I took part in a group show and my pictures were the only ones which were sold. The curator pocketed all of the money and paid her bank overdraft. A case of galleries disappearing with all artist's work is not unusual either. The exhibitions which the artist organises himself without the commercial gallery is a safer way to show work but has the drawback of the lack of contacts with the collectors of art. The assumption is that the gallery validates the artist's work. If it is shown in a gallery, it must be good! Commercial galleries take a very high percentage, 50%–80% or even more is the norm. While exhibiting in Paris, I met a young artist who had an agreement with his gallery which paid him a monthly salary but all the paintings he produced belonged to the gallery and he was not allowed to exhibit anywhere else. He seem very pleased with that arrangement.

In 1996, I had an exhibition in the Polish Cultural Institute in London. The title of the show was "THE MAN, THE LIGHT, THE SPACE"

A world of colour.
A play of imagination.
A powerful force.
An idea.
A shape, a symbol.
A joy of life in Nature's harmony,
in human existence.
Mystery, suffering and love.
Creations to see, think, and feel

*At the opening of the exhibition in the Polish Cultural Centre.
In front of the painting* Aspects of the World, *painting on cloth*

Three large rooms, well lit, gave me lots of space to exhibit a substantial number of recent work, 46 pieces in total.

Godfrey and I had to hang all the pictures ourselves and no help of any kind was provided by the institute. They covered the cost of the opening. Many visitors came to eat and drink. Some groups were spending time socialising and ignored completely the exhibition. One employee of the consulate came to me with the remark, *"I would rather buy a refrigerator than spend money on this wall hanging"* pointing at the big painting called *Aspects of the World*. I was very glad that a group of my friends came from Oxford and made the opening a pleasant occasion. The big drawback of having the exhibition in the institute was that it was what I call a "dead" place. While the same sort of cultural centre of France or Italy is buzzing with life with endless comings and goings of visitors, the Polish one is only open when the doorman wished to open the door and remained closed at weekends when the greatest number of visitors could come. This was more of a private club than an Art Centre.

In Halifax with baby Christopher

A great joyous event in our family was the announcement that Barbara and David were expecting their first child. They lived in Halifax, on the east coast of Canada. Barbara was working as a physiotherapist and biked in her spare time. She and Dave met while taking part in bike races, their great passion. They shared the love of nature, which in Canada, is unspoiled and wild, as I was going to discover on my subsequent visits there. Christopher was born in 1997 and shortly after, I went to assist in any way I could. Sitting with the baby on my lap was a great treat. I experienced such joy last when Barbara and Alexander were born. I had a few hand painted scarves with which I used to pacify little Christopher who like all babies loved looking at the movement of colours. It mesmerised him and after a while, his eyes closed and he was fast asleep. I made two trips to eastern Canada and each time I was astonished by the cleanliness of every town, every street and the coastal areas. Each street is always well marked and if I stood at the curb, cars inevitably stopped to let me cross. I wonder if the children are taught not to throw rubbish in the street or did the Canadians impose fines on those who create the mess as it happens in England. I can imagine that councils would make fortune in London imposing fines for the rubbish thrown in our streets. As to the naming of the streets, I despair. Arriving by car in Birmingham and looking for the name of a street is like looking for a needle in a haystack. The same applies in Croydon which must be the most annoying place on the planet to visit. If you want to know where you are, the only way is to walk into a shop or an office and ask because, the street map is of no use.

After 25 years of teaching in the School of Occupational Therapy, the retirement loomed and, ahead of me, much more time for art. Opening the studio to the public each year was very time consuming in terms of organising the house into an exhibition place, a gallery. In one bedroom, I made a photographic display while downstairs I showed the collection of paintings, drawings and prints. Sometimes, the garden also had unexpected things to see. One year, after the official opening of the Oxford Art Week by the famous and charismatic Richard Demarco, he visited my studio. He knew nothing about me but as soon as he crossed the threshold he exclaimed: "*I am in Poland!*" This, to me was the most unexpected, spontaneous remark since I never thought of my art as being Polish in any way! Even now, years later I do not believe that there is such a thing as 'national art'. I wish that I had time to discuss it with Demarco but he had little time while doing rounds of some studios before returning to his native Edinburgh. This was going to be one of my last Open Studio in Oxford because soon my life was going to change drastically. After 35 years of living in my house in Summertown a neighbour from hell moved next door and my normal life became greatly disturbed. Not able to find resolution to the problem, and discovering what an ass the law is I made a decision to move to London.

Alexander's friends, Ana and Jo Balance knew the house well and wanted to buy it. They were not worried about the problems with the disturbed neighbour.

I knew that leaving Oxford and all my friends was not going to be easy, in fact I expected that my life once again will have to change very much. Alexander who specialised in the Rehabilitation Technology, had a permanent job in London where his wife also worked.

I expected that sooner or later they will start a family and I might be useful when the baby arrives!

Looking for a house in southwest London, I was once again walking the streets of Tooting where once upon a time, I lived in

Studio 54, London

Lucien Road. This was no longer the same city. Although the houses looked the same there was a difference, many were very neglected and there was a lot of rubbish around. People seemed to throw on the pavement everything which they no longer needed. One could equip totally a house with beds, settees, chairs and tables to name but a few of the objects clattering the pavements from time to time. Many houses were rented and as usual, left unloved by the accidental occupants. In 1957 after the morning rush hour, the streets were reasonably empty of humanity while in the year 1998 the streets seem full of humanity obviously not working.

I wondered, how did they keep their body and soul together without having to work?

Finding a house in the area not far from my son, was not easy. On average, it takes six months, to look, to deal with the purchase and to move. Many were for sale but every one seem so soulless. The house had to have a potential for making it into a studio and the garden must face south. There were many unloved and neglected houses, vastly overpriced till I noticed in the window of an estate agent a modest, yellow brick, nineteen fifties house which the estate agent said was wrong for me and very reluctantly, agreed for me to view. The back of the house was facing south – Hurrah! And it was

*Painting on
the wall in
Studio 54*

not too expensive. I moved in 1998 with my old cat Bilbo. As soon
as we walked in, Bilbo found a space under the staircase to hide and
keep out of the way of endless boxes and pictures being moved into
the house. Bilbo hated the journey from Oxford in Alexander's Land
Rover. As soon as the removal van deposited its load, Alexander
insisted on putting up my bed and making sure that the basics were
unpacked and in place. The cat stayed hidden while I wandered
round my new garden thinking how I would design this new space.
My box with paints and brushes was well marked amongst the packages and as soon as I organised the utensils in the kitchen, I started
painting my first picture (never mind boxes standing around waiting
to be unpacked). If I could paint, I was in the right place, the house
was No. 54 and I was going to call it STUDIO 54. This was a famous studio in New York attracting some well-known American
artists – perhaps this new home would bring me peace and luck!
The cat slowly got out of his hiding place and walked round the garden paying special attention to the small pond. There were some
fishes in the pond and I knew that I had to find a home for them.

For the next six days he was kept inside the house, to get used to
our new home. In time small alterations in the house had to take
place. I did not appreciate the various tiles on the floor with a
butterfly print on them and the paper boarder on the walls with the

My Garden World, *acrylic on board*

same colourful image. I was extremely lucky when one day I went
to the big store with tiles to inquire about plain tiles which needed
replacing. I showed the sales person the sample of the required one
but he nodded that these come from Spain and he never had them in
his store. Just at that moment, a man standing behind told me that
he was the one who tiled some of my floors a few years back and
that he has a bucket full of them left over. How happy was I in the
knowledge that the butterflies will be replaced! We decided with
Godfrey that a few weeks of separation was in order to allow me to
organise my new life. When he next visited me, he saw the new
home of mine and agreed the plan of a house-warming party to
which I would invite many of my old friends from Oxford. What
joy it was, short lived but at least my friends could picture me from
now on in my new environment. Soon, I had my first Open Studio
in Streatham, by invitation only. I knew that it was not safe to open
it to the general public. My large, front window in the new studio
was a good space for placing a small exhibition of sculptures and a
painting. As soon as my first display was finished, the bell rung and
in the doorway stood a tall, young black man saying *"I like your
sculptures very much, but if I make love to you, you will make even
more beautiful ones"*! I couldn't stop laughing at this unexpected
reaction to my window display. I had to decline his offer and
explained why it would have been out of place. I could see his disappointment but in the end he accepted my decision and I never saw
him again.

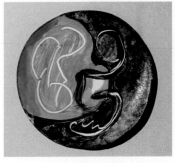 

*Painting
on plates*

15. Cathedrals, Victoria

The beauty of your work is rooted in the reality of the earth but it raises the earth to heaven where God transforms it.

Sister Wendy Beckett

Sister Wendy Beckett is a nun who loves art and has written a few books about spirituality in paintings. A few times when I heard her speaking, I was full of admiration for the great sensitivity and very Christian interpretation of pictures which she studied. Full of admiration for her scholarly studies, I send an etching, a present for her convent. She liked its content and send me a letter from which the above quotation came.

The year was 2000 and a special one for me. I embarked on project of creating three drawings on each day of that new millennium year. I called it "Pages of Time" and did not miss a single day. Each month the drawings were placed in a separate portfolio and Barbara's old trunk became its storage place. There is continuum in these drawings and towards the end of 2000 the drawings became triptychs.

The opportunity to take part in an exhibition with Elzbieta Stanhope was a welcomed one.

The Chelsea Gallery in the Old Church Street was going to show her very unusual pots decorated with female faces reminding me of Greek frescoes. I would show paintings and drawings and call my exhibition "Music And More" – 30 pieces altogether. Our work looked well together and I was pleased when two pastel drawings were purchased by a girl from Thailand.

Godfrey was very pleased when I told him about an idea which was born when I visited, for the first time, an English cathedral.

Canterbury Cathedral,
single copy print

This happened shortly after I met George who was a very keen photographer particularly of old historical buildings, temples and other objects of art. He took me to Canterbury where I was bowled over by the majesty and history of the cathedral. It was still the time when parking the car in the centre of any town was possible. We spent a long time learning about the history of the cathedral, George was photographing parts of the interior where the sunlight found its way in and created a mysterious atmosphere. When we returned to the car and started driving off passers-by waved to us in great urgency pointing at the roof. We eventually stopped and discovered that George left his Leica M3, a very expensive camera, on the roof of the car. The memory of that first adventure, the beauty of the cathedral planted a thought in my mind of wanting to make sometime in the future a collection of cathedral images. It took the next 35 years before the idea came back to me. Godfrey was very enthusiastic and after I studied and planned the project, we went for weekend trips to visit the cathedrals which interested me. I chose five – Canterbury, St Paul's, Wells, Peterborough and Lichfield. Each one completely different in its

*Drawing on the subject
of a cathedral*

Master's degree graduation day for Alexander

design, all of them built in the centre of town. The only area which has been drastically changed is that of St Paul's where modern architecture now dominates its surroundings. For the next year, I concentrated on the subject creating a limited edition of seven copies of each one. Having finished it, I felt the need to continue the subject but crate another collection of drawings about the cathedrals. I found that the two separate and different images work well side by side. I was hoping to exhibit all of them at St Paul's where exhibitions are often held. The committee unfortunately did not approve my proposal. However I gave one of the collections to St Cross College in memory of George who was its founder member.

My house in Streatham is a short walk from the home of my son and his wife. When their son was born in 2000, I knew that they would appreciate my help and so it was that six months after Freddie was born his mother, Frauke, returned to work and I had the wonderful opportunity to collect him from the nursery and take

Vancouver Island beaches

Driftwood from Victoria,
Singularity *(above) and* Family *(left)*

home. While he was growing, and when he did not fall asleep on the way home, we had lovely time stopping at the park and playing. Mothering was always a great joy for me and it is reflected in some of my paintings and drawings. When Barbara's second child was born, I went to Canada to be part of that happy family. Bianca was born on the west coast of Canada, in Victoria, Vancouver Island. Barbara and her partner Dave Maclaud, moved from the east coast in order to have a better climate and longer seasons of sunny weather for biking, their passion. This is a most beautiful and unspoiled part of the world where we took many walks along the wild beaches on which, discarded by the sea, remnants of cedar forests cover the shore. It looked like a never-ending sculpture park. I could not resist picking up some, beautifully polished by the sea, pieces of cedar. Inevitably my suitcase was full of these precious pieces which were turned into three dimensional compositions upon my return home. I also worked with these while in Victoria and left the finished compositions in various gardens. Canadians care about their environment and it is always a great privilege to be there and a terrible shock when I return to the extremely messy world in which I now live. So much disregard for trees and for nature. It will always be a great sadness for me. This is no longer the England I saw in 1957 when I arrived for the first time. Each time I returned from a trip abroad I delighted in the beauty of cared-for nature Much has changed since that time.

Christopher and Bianca, Barbara's children are very lucky to grow up in the part of the world where the air is pure and the nature unspoiled!

Both my children appreciated my creative output and like to have my pictures on the walls of their homes. Barbara suggested that we should turn her clinic into a gallery for a few days, to have an exhibition of my art. This involved a major revolution in the orderly clinical space which she created and improved over many years.

Barbara has an amazing amount of energy, and once she makes a decision nothing will stop her from achieving her goal. It took a few days to remove every trace of clinic and create a gallery. The first exhibition was called "The Old And The New" and two years later the second one "Love and Music".

Having many patients and friends was most useful and invitations were sent out. Dave built a gazebo at the entrance to the exhibition where visitors had wine while the food was placed on the tables in the exhibition rooms. The clinic became an Oak Crest Gallery, just for a few days! People who came were genuinely interested in art. It is not often that visitors wish to talk about the exhibits and I was pleasantly surprised by the genuine interest. Most questioning related to the technique which in my art is often a mixture of using different tools and different base on which the image is created. It was the most delightful opening I ever had thanks to my daughter's hard work. Returning the space back to its clinical purpose was just as time consuming as creating a gallery.

Since my childhood, I liked drawing and one day, a thought struck me that I could draw my telephone conversations.

While I am talking on the telephone I react differently to each conversation. It depends on the mood, on the subject and my relationship with the person I am talking with. This ongoing project has so far resulted in over a thousand drawings, each one as different as the conversation and the time involved. Although all drawings are spontaneous, there is a repetition of emerged pattern

Talking on the telephone and drawing the conversation (above)
and six of the thousand telephone conversations (below)

connected with a particular person. For a psychologist this would be a fascinating subject to analyse and come up with interesting theories. Communication is currently an important topic since the new technology promotes constant communication between people. Drawing for me is a necessity, it keeps my mental balance, my sanity. It was Graham Greene who said once that he cannot understand how a human being can stay sane without some creativity. I totally agree with him. Perhaps, writing by hand was one such creative activity. Using handwritten notes, people were not just communicating but also conveying a little bit of the individual personality. A handwritten note is much more personal and humanity is in danger of losing the need to write by hand. Although I have not any memory of my first lesson in writing, I have a proof that at the age of three my father led my hand in writing a letter to Father Christmas with request for some toys, ensuring him that I was a good girl and ate my dinners! Both my sister and I were encouraged to write neatly from an early age. I wonder what influences the final style of person's writing – when it becomes sloping or upright, italic, angular, elegant or slapdash. I have kept for over sixty years letters written by my parents, my children and friends. All of them are sort of documents and represent the uniqueness of the person who wrote them. The handwriting changes with age and the use of different pens also influences the resulting text. The biro slides on paper fast while the felt tip and fountain pens give small resistance and allow for greater control. To write anything by hand can be very creative, sensuous and individual. It is as unique and intimate as making a drawing. It is just you, a pen, a piece of paper and your thoughts which you wish to convey to someone. The uniqueness of it represents your personality, I am sure that the keyboard will never be a substitute for the beauty of handwriting. My handwriting changes with my mood, sometimes it is straight and rounded at other times it is slanting from left to right and seem to run! It gives me as much joy as making a drawing. Looking at the visitor's book from the many exhibitions, is most interesting.

it several times, all very in ...
that can wait till I'm ba...
before not only in psycho...
management. Most of it...
and how this pertained to ...

I love your letterhead unique and ...
The weather is starting to get cold...
coming to a fabulous dinner with ...

pozwolić na kupienie
nowego. A czy nie mores...
posłuchać u są'rodów ?
Czy jesteś b. samotna ?
Czy Tobie ta samotność
nie dobiła ? Przecież
wszystkich przyjaciół
zostałaś w Londynie.
Napisz mi jak

kochania moja, przede wszystk...
dziękuję Ci za takie miłe dzieci
u was w Oxfordzie. Aleksander
wyrośli na przecute dzieci i tak...

LANDO - tempo jes...
... - moja swoj...
... śnieg i en zapew...
... zbijały się bu ...
... po solic pann'ę
... ej Ci byłaś, or ...
... udane masz Dzie...
... satysfakcję - ...
... stygn uśmiechem...
... W okunics...
Jest struktura...

małżeński nie porzysz...
żadnych corn flaków, kakao itp., bo
my mamy tutaj to wszystko i to co
płacić b. drogą opłatę pocztowa za potem
cło — mamy dobre przetwory zbożowe
jak dętą ryż, dętą kukurydzę, a kakao

This provides a marvellous opportunity
to taste and learn about many different
wines under the guidance of experts!
My sport is keeping me very fit and
my social-life, quite busy. Studies are
quite sometimes difficult and tend t

Handwriting by the different members of my family

Every single person is different and so is their style of writing. The difference between the restless and calm person or the rushed one and the impatient are reflected in their little note or just the signature. To me this is an endless fascination.

My children were surrounded by my art from an early age. Used to my semi-abstracted style, they accepted my personal and individual version of life as I understood and saw it. My father was perplexed by it, whenever I showed him reproductions on many visits home. Being a scientist, he liked pictures which he could understand – representing realistically the world. His approach to music was the same, he enjoyed the classical and traditional compositions. When, once sitting on a flight next to a man who introduced himself: "*I am Lutoslawski*", it meant little to my father. The man was a very famous, contemporary Polish composer who was most surprised when introducing himself did not cause the expected awe. My mother's approach to art was quite different. She did not need to see a representation in a picture but was responding to colour and the atmosphere. Because I had frequent questions about my art I had to put together the following introductory text titled "Some Thoughts on Art":

Art is about discovering and creating a new world. Artist's work is a constant search for his or her own expression of the physical and spiritual reality in which we live.

The painter has the task of transforming the three dimensional world onto a flat surface.

Like a man who operates a computer, he can use a system of codes or symbols which help him to make the thing work.

He also has at his disposal colour, line, form and texture.

However, every technique has its limitations, and cannot do justice to the vastness of the world of images, feelings and ideas which are the driving force behind the creative process. The creative force which is very powerful and the source of an artist's work, leads him into the unknown world of discovery and learning, resulting in unique and sometimes strange pictures.

To understand the often unusual painting or sculpture can be as difficult as the initial glance at a computer screen or a page of short handwriting. It means very little to us except that it can excite our imagination by its pure originality, by the colour or the shape of its symbols. Perhaps it is meant to show us something different from what we already know. This newness and originality can suggest another way of seeing, understanding and feeling about the visible and invisible world around us. If we give it a chance it can enrich our lives with a new dimension and a new vision.

This text was well received by those who needed help with viewing the contemporary art and the visitors to my studio during the Oxford Art Week.

Godfrey's health was deteriorating, but he was a fighter who never missed an opportunity to learn more about the latest treatment for his kind of cancer. He was getting weaker but in spite of not feeling strong he was planning our next expedition somewhere into a glorious landscape. Our many holidays included a trip to Knossos, to the Swiss Alps to the Greek Islands, Vienna, Budapest, Barcelona and a special tour of Scotland. When he had to give up sailing and sell the lovely Pegasus 800 I was in tears. We both loved getting away from humanity, sailing into secluded creeks overnight and being awaken by the seabirds. Curlew's call, even at night is a mellow whistle *"curlee"*. At low tide, the mudflats attract many different birds who are oblivious to the presence of a boat stuck on the mud!

Godfrey was always enthusiastic about a possibility of another exhibition and looking forward to the openings which were not my favourite part of it. I am not the only artist disliking private views. Picasso avoided openings regularly. One of my last exhibitions in Oxford was to take place in the Oxford Said Business School which had a very big, well-lit hall used for conferences thus allowing for a large audience to view the show. I called the exhibition "ABSTRACT to FIGURATIVE." All paintings and drawings in the show, were created between 1998 and 2005.

I had planned exactly how and where each work was going to hang and Alexander who took all my work to Oxford, had no problem in hanging them up. I always marvel at his talent to

  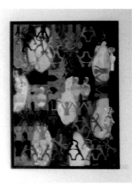

Today,
Tomorrow,
The Future,
*three paintings
on board
(above)*

*Part of the
painting (left)*

Painting on the subject of 9-11

understand a problem and see the quickest and the best solution to solve it. Working together, the exhibition of 30 paintings, drawings as well as some of "The Telephone Conversations" were put up very quickly and looked well together. Many of my friends came to the opening to see what I was working on since leaving Oxford and moving to London. Janine Alton a reviewer for the *Oxford Times* came to interview me on a day when only a few visitors were around. She was an exceptionally insightful reviewer and it was a pleasure to have a discussion with her. It always surprised me that Oxford's press did not have an art reviewer who would be able to convey their understanding of the artist's work. Describing the art is not enough. My visitor's book from that exhibition is full of interesting comments written in a more or less legible writing. As always, looking at the messages, I wonder what the author of it looks like, my fascination with the fellow humans is as always important.

Art

MALGORZATA BIALOKOZ SMITH: SAID BUSINESS SCHOOL

Malgorzata — she won't mind my calling her 'Margaret' from now on — lived in Oxford for many years and was a regular presence in the city's Artweeks. In 1998 she moved to London and her show at the Said Business School (till September 18) represents new work from the years since. I say 'represents' because she is a most prolific and varied artist and the couple of dozen pieces on view, fascinating and thoughtful though they certainly are, give only a taste of her total production — there's also a portfolio with more examples, well worth looking at.

The paintings — oil, acrylic, mixed media — are well-described in the show's title, *Abstract to Figurative*. They are charged with hints and mysteries, not abstruse or esoteric but leaving the viewer to find a way through their symbols, recurrent images and patterns. Margaret grew up in Catholic Poland, and we can see many icons of the church in her work. *Pieta*, a 2005 painting inspired by the suffering mothers of Beslan, echoes both in its title and in the grieving faces one of the great motifs of Calvary.

It may not be altogether fanciful to see in religious art her frequent, and unusual, use of the triptych. There are several striking examples here. The large-scale sequence *Today, Tomorrow, The Future* shows similar tiny figures, touching, battling, dancing, against backgounds moving from predominant crimson through grey, ochre and sepia to dark, the vibrant colour movement suggesting Margaret's fear of humanity's self-destruction. So too does *The earth is changing*, where she also suggest her disquiet at the increasing homogeneity of modern life. Add to these her take on 9/11, with Munch-like open-mouthed screams and the livid parallel lines of skyscrapers, and the show and the artist might sound grim. Nothing could be further from the case. Margaret's paintings of *Motions of Love* are tender, her *Music of Love* (*left*) is jokey and her *Music of the Spheres* (*detail, right*) is intriguing. Her palette makes a firm statement without ever becoming strident.

And she is alarmingly perceptive. There's a panel of bold portrait heads, almost cartoons, sketched on a return visit to Warsaw in May. And a series of her latest idea — doodles into art, designs, or hints of personality jotted down in pencil, pen or colour during phone conversations, all bearing the name of the 'sitter'. Definitely a lively mind.

Jeannine Alton

Review of the exhibition

Godfrey and I usually spent weekends together at his home in Wendlebury near Oxford or in London at my house. His garden needed care and there were many public paths outside the village where we walked for many miles. In London we went to concerts, the Proms were our favourite ones as well as the opera, if the production did not contain contemporary vulgarity. When the singers sat on loos or an explicit sex was taking place our sensitivity kept us away from attending such performance. Godfrey usually rung the Colosseum to investigate the production before buying tickets. On his eightieth birthday celebration, he invited a group of special friends to the performance of *The Fledermaus*. He provided the minibus transport to take us in comfort from Oxford to London and back home. Everybody enjoyed this generous treat. When he suffered two bouts of pneumonia, I stayed with him till he was reasonably fit again. I saw that each time his body was responding less and less to treatment but his indomitable spirit never let him down till the third time. He rung me up on the morning of the day when once again the ambulance was called to take him to the John Radcliffe Hospital. I was going to join him at the hospital as soon as I could get there by the usual coach. He wanted to hear a joke while waiting. We shared jokes very often when we spoke on the phone every day, twice, at 8.30 am and 5.30 pm. This was a joke which made him laugh in spite of the fact that he had great difficulty breathing. "*Three scholars are waiting at a bus stop talking when the bus arrives and the door opens. They are deep in some discussion and take no notice till the driver calls – 'all aboard!' Two of the men jump on and the bus drives off. The third man stands with his head down, looking rather sad. A young man standing next to him says, 'Sir, I would not worry, two out of three is a good average'. The man looks at him and says, 'you are right, but they came to see me off'.*"

This was the last time that I heard Godfrey laugh. Later on I had a phone call from the hospital asking me to collect some eye drops from his house which he forgot to take with him. It meant a much longer journey time before I could reach the hospital. I was never again to see him conscious because by the time I arrived to his bedside he was barely breathing.

I was with him for the next three hours, talking to him and looking for a response to no avail. When his heart stopped beating at 6 pm, my hope of hearing his voice for the last time was gone. Some years earlier, Godfrey and I were at the bedside of his dying mother. She was drifting slowly in and out of consciousness but suddenly before she died she looked at Godfrey and said "*Help to make this world a better place*". I wondered what would have been Godfrey's last words if only I arrived in time, before he lost consciousness.

It was the end of 25 years of love and devotion, of sharing all joys and sorrows. I left the hospital feeling utterly devastated and engulfed in total loneliness. Ahead of me were two bus journeys to his house in Wendlebury where the tweeting sparrows were the only sign of life. I needed the silent time of emptiness and despair

Symbols of Life

which inevitably is following the death of a close person. I had to deal with my own feeling of devastation before facing the world with the awful news of Godfrey's death. I walked around his garden, talked to the birds and the trees which Godfrey loved. The old lilac trees which every springtime filled his garden with colour and scent, the majestic, old apple tree which gave him wonderful fruit every year. I knew that my children will help me in this awful, sad time and Barbara will come from far away Victoria to be with me. The college will also offer help to the man who was always taking part in its life. The daughters, no doubt will want to come to his house, to take some objects to remind them of the time when they had to visit him throughout their childhood.

Every life consists of achievements and disappointments, about joys and sadness. The 25 years which we shared without living under the same roof were punctuated with exciting time of many discoveries in different worlds. We were never bored in each other's company. At the end of every year, Godfrey received from me a photographic record of our time together. These pictures are the fragments of the continuum of our life and will always remind me of the happy times we shared. All these thoughts went through my mind while I was aware of the need to inform my children and his children of Godfrey's death. Sitting by the telephone, I was well aware of the fact that from now on my life would once more change. I had a great responsibility to deal with his estate and follow his wishes entrusted to me. My children were not only a great comfort but also extremely helpful. I was hoping that my usual creative urge will help me through this sad time but it was not to be. For the next 19 months I was unable to draw or to paint. It was the longest time in my life without being involved in my art. Throughout my life, the experience as well as the historical events, fed my artistic output. This time I seem to have entered a different phase and have to accept possibility of never returning to my world of art. Time seems to go

Wooden blocks

faster and I am aware of its passing more than ever before. Duchamp, the famous French artist said *"My capital is time not money."* He was right, every minute of our life, is lived only once. Godfrey entrusted me the job of sorting out his estate and his will. This complex and time consuming occupation, took 19 months.

I became aware for the first time, how important it is to put one's life in order especially when one reaches the old age. My large output of art, which belongs to my children needs to be catalogued

(some of it discarded) and the collection of my parents' letters and photographs requires many hours of selection. Perhaps in the future I might once again find excitement facing a blank canvas or a piece of paper and the flow of that powerful creative energy will entice me to create something new. For the time being the healing process has to take its course.

Dream of Love, *monotype*

16. Our Feline Friends

A very charming "interlude" – I certainly think you should keep it – it says more about your family very appropriately.
Dorothy

During my travels round the world, I met many different people and also – animals. My favourite were the cats always different from our western domesticated pets. Most of the encountered cats were almost wild, living freely, feeding on whatever they could find and often rather neglected. The shapes of these cats were reminiscent of the Egyptian sculptures in their elegant slimness and distinct pose. In Egypt 950 BC cats were venerated as sacred. Our domesticated pets are usually rounded with rich shiny fur which they like keeping clean.

After Ika and I left home, cat number one entered their life.

Not far from their flat, in the park which was the beginning of extensive forests, was an animal sanctuary for cats and dogs, unwanted by the public. It was a very primitive place consisting of two enclosures open to the rain and wind. The dogs barked almost non-stop in constant agitation while the cats were all curled up, trying to keep warm, in the separate enclosure. My mother often went for a walk by this place and inevitably, felt sorry for the plight of all the animals. During one such walk, on a frosty morning her attention was drawn to a small, black kitten who sat by the fence meowing in desperation. Without hesitation, she decided to rescue this small creature with white paws. My father did not mind and together they devoted much care and love to bring the kitten to health. She in return adored my parents and expressed it in many different ways. My mother wrote a long essay about Pussol – the

Pussol, who adored my mother (left) but hated visitors (above)

name they gave her. Pussol did not tolerate visitors, expressing her annoyance by first loud meowing then, attacking the legs of the newcomer. This was most embarrassing for my parents who eventually learned to put their cat behind closed door for the duration of the visit. She loved going for a walk with my father and walked like a little dog on a lead. The local dogs kept a safe distance knowing her aggressive temper and readiness to attack if necessary. Father was a celebrity, walking with the cat on the lead. While taking his daily, constitutional walk, often with Pussol he picked up with the spiky end of his walking stick, any encountered rubbish. He always said that the care for the environment is everybody's duty. One of the favourite excursion of my parents was a short trip to the Tuchom Lake. Pussol, of course went with them and was allowed to walk around freely, never venturing too far. One day, he simply went off and the parents were very concerned for his safety. They put up notices offering a reward and every day drove to the lake and surrounding woods in hope of finding Pussol. Their persistence paid off. One day after calling her, they heard the faint "miou" and a very wet and bedraggled cat run towards them. This must have been the biggest adventure of her otherwise protected life. She must have encountered a tom cat because it became obvious that she was pregnant. It was a sad adventure which ended tragically. The birth followed but she died shortly in great pain. Her kittens were very sick and did not survive. For my parents, this was very traumatic time, seeing the cat's suffering and not being able to help. My mother wrote the story of Pussol's life as she understood it. There was a great bond between her and the little cat rescued on a frosty day.

Many months passed and the day came when she had once again the courage to walk by the cat and dog sanctuary. Having passed the noisy place she became aware of being followed.

A young, bedraggled ginger cat was following her. She walked faster in hope of losing the cat to no avail. He insisted on following her as close as possible like a little dog.

All the way, across the road and up the steps to the house. He was determined to find a new home and in his eyes, this lady looked promising. This was the beginning of another love affair between the lady and the feline friend who was called Puss by my parents.

His character was completely different, he showed great affection towards everybody and as soon as somebody sat down, he was settling on their lap. When, one day, I was sitting by the typewriter Puss jumped up and curled himself round my shoulders like a big warm collar. When my mother died, Puss followed my father all the time as if trying to say, "*I am your companion now*"! If my father was not well and lying in bed, Puss would sit on top of him and purring loudly gazed insistently into my father's eyes, willing him to get well again. It was great sadness for my father when Puss died of

Puss loved everybody!

kidney failure. Both cats were buried in the woods from which, many years earlier, they had come – to become a happy part of my parents' lives.

Shortly after George died, a friend offered us a white kitten. We fell in love with the bundle of white fur and the children called him Snowy.

Snowy lived a double life of a hunter at night and a purring, sleepy softie during the day.

His whiteness prevented him from catching a single bird but his nightly escapades were more successful and an occasional mouse was found on the doorstep as an offering.

It was on a Bonfire Night that Snowy suffered serious injury. We

Barbara with Snowy

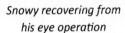

*Snowy recovering from
his eye operation*

will never know how and where it happened. We found him in the morning on our doorstep – his fur was singed and one of his eyes was covered with a huge bloody scab. His eye was damaged and had to be removed. Snowy gradually got used to having one eye but his judgement of distance was never correct. Jumping onto something resulted in misjudging the distance and falling to the ground. He was very hurt when we laughed at his mishaps and walked away in dignified way as if saying: *"shame on you all"*. My father was one member of our family who understood Snowy's predicament. After his detached retina operation, he had a fall which resulted in losing sight on the operated eye. Like Snowy, he also had a problem in judging distances and drove his car with great care, giving much space between his car and the one in front. My father coped with the situation and continued his academic work and Snowy in time, returned to his nightly escapades. A few years later while out at night, he went to the neighbours' garden and while trying to have a drink from their pond, fell in, got tangled in the protective netting and drowned. It was very tragic because we all loved this very calm and friendly cat.

One Christmas, a few years later, my children gave me a very special present – a black kitten. He came from a commune in East Oxford and was obviously very lively and quite terrified of his new surroundings. He came to me with the name Bilbo. His other siblings were also called with names from Tolkien's world of fantasy. Bilbo settled well into his new home but it became soon quite obvious that he was a hunter and much more aggressive than Snowy. Robins make their nest low in the bushes which is easy for a cat to destroy. When the bird made such a nest, I saw how Bilbo spent

Bilbo chasing a spider

many hours sitting near and observing the robin. I had to build a big structure with elaborate netting to prevent Bilbo from getting near the nest. I kept an eye on the nest and on Bilbo until the fledglings flew out. I suspect that the cat understood my annoyance and took my shouting seriously, because he never came with dead birds and I never saw him chasing them. The day when Alex drove Bilbo and me to Streatham was very disruptive for the little cat. When we arrived, he quickly found himself a place to hide and wait for all the commotion to end. Only when all was quiet he ventured out to investigate his new home. I carried him around the house and garden and explained the new space to him. At the age of 16, he became ill and his kidneys were infected. He lost weight and looked unhappy. One night he went away and most probably wished to die alone.

All four cats, the feline friends, Pussol, Puss, Snowy and Bilbo were part of our family and we cherished their presence and their love for us.

My garden now has a large flock of sparrows established in the rampant pyracantha bush, which vibrates with tweeting and movement. A robin makes his nest every springtime and a red woodpecker visits the feeder very often. A flock of long-tailed, blue and great tits, visits the garden also. The many house sparrows chirp from morning till evening and love having a bath in the pond or in the bowl of water for drinking. The males are more colourful and aggressive never wanting to share their food. The young ones, in the spring learn how to have a bath. It takes them a lot of time before they are brave enough to jump in the water. Birds inspired me to make a collection of drawings. It is my interpretation of the image and the movement.

Those Amongst Us, *painting, second prize at the four-counties open painting competition*

My Final Words

The story of my life is like a picture in which the dark parts and the light ones represent both sadness and joy. Writing this memoir allowed me to travel back in time and encounter once more the important moments which shaped my life. I met many people on that journey. Friendships, some were lasting, others, like a wind, died down over time. My art led me through the rough times, trage-dies and disappointments which sunk deep into my imagination. I was determined to continue painting and drawing whenever there was a free moment.

I feel grateful for all the opportunities that I had, my life has been blessed in very many ways. My parents' unconditional love, care and encouragement became the most important example. *"Be productive, creative, live for others and stay positive!"*. This was their advice, their life's motto.

My children, Alexander and Barbara became my greatest joy.

I watched them grow, to become a very special, talented and pro-fessional people who care for others. Their world, and the world of their children, Christopher, Bianca and Frederick, is completely different from the world in which I grew up. The technological rush of consumerism can endanger our culture of values, insights and opportunities.

The uncontrolled growth of the world population and climatic changes partially resulting from the constant destruction of the environment, are the huge problems which my grandchildren's generation will have to deal with.

I strongly believe in creativity as a dynamic force which resists conformity, challenges assumptions, helps to make sense of every-thing and leads to self-realisation of an individual.

While looking back at the historical events which I witnessed –

the landing on the moon was probably the most spectacular. The future on our Earth, might be even more unexpected and interesting. Humanity will employ more and more robots and have more and more time which, if used for creative pursuits and sport, will enrich life and help people stay sane!

Writing this "selective memoir" would not have happen without the support and encouragement of my children and the patience on the part of my friends, Sheila and Jo Olliver, Dorothy Horgan, Malgosia Vermes and Joan O'Sullivan, who gave their time to read some chapters, insisting that I keep my English–Polish language unchanged: *"this is your language"*!

For their assistance and help, I am most grateful.

Malgorzata,
November 2015,
London

A Chronology of the Life and Times of our Family

1867–1918 Heronim & Eleonora Tilgner in Berlin, the first Polish mail order catalogue published in Berlin

26 November 1904 Damazy Tilgner born near Poznan

3 January 1909 Halina Hauffe born in Poznan

10 November 1912 George Bialokoz born in Carskie Siolo

4 August 1914 First World War

1917 Russian Revolution, beginning of Socialism (repudiation of the idea of ownership).

1918 Heronim, Eleonora and their five children return to Poznan. He dies of heart attack.

1928–1931 Damazy & Halina work in the USA

1932 they meet in Gdynia and marry in 1934 in Warsaw

10 September 1937 Malgorzata Tilgner born in Warsaw

3 September 1939 Germans invade Poland, Second World War

1 February 1941 Ika Tilgner the second daughter is born.

9 May 1945 The end of the war and the start of the Russian occupation

1945 family starts new life in Bydgoszcz, having lost their houses in Gdynia and Warsaw.

August 1945 the atom bomb dropped on Nagasaki and Hiroshima.

Summer 1951 Father starts professorship in Gdansks Technical University, family moves to Sopot

1956 end of Technical School of Plastic Arts, start of the Academy of Arts in Gdansk.

13 September 1958 arrived in London

1960 National Diploma in Design in St Martin's School of Art

1961–1962 Teaching in the West of England College of Art in Bristol

1962 married George Bialokoz, moved to Oxford and became Margaret Bialokoz

15 February 1963 Alexander George born in Oxford

5 May 1964 Barbara Alexandra born in Oxford

1966–1967 sabbatical leave, George and the family visits universities in the USA

13 January 1968 Prof. Dr Ing. Damazy Tilgner expelled from the university in Gdansk

1969 Apollo lands on the Moon

1969 March George Bialokoz dies

1971 Ika married Peter Schreiner in Oslo

1971 Malgorzata married Neil Patrick Smith

1973 November beginning of 25 years of teaching at the Dorset House School of Occupational Therapy in Oxford

1976–1981 Children at the Cherwell Secondary School

2 May 1980 Neil died after eight years of cancer

1980 "Solidarity" movement in Poland

1981 the launch of the Open Studios in Oxford, the first in GB and martial law imposed in Poland

1982 Adult Education Course, Nottingham

1982–1985 Barbara at Southampton University and later at Dalhausie University in Canada studying Biochemistry and Physiotherapy.

1985 Barbara in Kobe, Japan, volleyball, World Students Games

1986 Barbara plays volleyball at Calgary University, Canada

1986 Malgorzata's trip round the World

1987 Alex at the Central London Polytechnic & World Students Games

1987 Alex and Barbara play volleyball at the World Student Games in Zagreb

1987 May met Godfrey Tyler

2 February 1988 Mother died of cancer

1989 Alex plays volleyball in Finland & the fall of Berlin Wall, the Iron Curtain

1990 Alex met Frauke Schulze

1991–1994 Barbara at Dalhausie University in Canada

1991 Collapse of the Soviet Union & the beginning of the internet

1992 Prof. Dr D. J. Tilgner – Doctor Honoris Causa – Gdansk Technical University

1992, honoris causa for my father from the Gdańsk University of Technology

1993 last of the Russian troops leave Poland & Formation of the European Union

1995 Alex at Queen Mary – Special Seating Rehabilitation Engineer

30 September 1995 Wedding of Alexander and Frauke

19 February 1997 Father died of cancer

1997 I wrote *Art through Discovery, Discovery through Art*, a resume of my teaching of art.

10 April 1997 Barbara's and David's son, Christopher, born and on the 14 September 1998 Bianca Paris, born in Victoria

1998 Malgorzata moves to London

23 July 2000 Frederick, son of Frauke and Alex born

2001 Alex joins Kings College as a research assistant for two years

2004 Poland becomes member of the European Union, mass exodus of the population.

2004 Alex returns to Roehampton

2012 June Godfrey died of cancer

List of Exhibitions

ONE PERSON EXHIBITIONS
1971 English-Speaking Union, Oxford-drawings – paintings
1975 Playhouse Gallery, Oxford – paintings
1977 County Museum, Woodstock – batiks
1977 International Language Centre, Paris, France – paintings and monoprints
1978 Blasbortv. Oslo, Norway – monoprints
1980 Thames Gallery, Henley-on-Thames – mixed media
1982 Balliol, Green, Wadham Colleges, Oxford – batiks
1984 Templeton College, Kennington, Oxford – paintings
1986 Sheraton Gallery, Karachi, Pakistan – prints
1987 Centre for the study of Spirituality and the Arts, London – etchings
1989 The Hill Gallery, Hampstead, London – retrospective
1992 The Heffers Gallery, Cambridge – prints and paintings
1992 Museum of Contemporary Art, Radom, Poland – works on paper
1993 Triada Gallery, Sopot, Poland – triptychs on hand made paper
1996 Polish Cultural Institute, London – paintings, drawings
2000 Bartley Drey Gallery, London – paintings, drawings
2008 Oak Crest Gallery, Victoria, Canada – mixed media
2010 Oak Crest Gallery, Victoria, Canada – paintings and prints

Mothers of the World 1, *painting on paper*